Good Times at
GREEN LAKE

Good Times at
GREEN LAKE

································

RECIPES FOR
Seattle's Favorite Park

SUSAN BANKS AND CAROL ORR

Washington State University Press
Pullman, Washington

Washington State University Press
PO Box 645910
Pullman, Washington 99164-5910
Phone: 800-354-7360
Fax: 509-335-8568
E-mail: wsupress@wsu.edu
Web site: www.wsu.edu/wsupress
© 2000 by the Board of Regents of Washington State University
All rights reserved
First printing 2000

Library of Congress Cataloging-in-Publication Data

Banks, Susan, 1954-
  Good times at Green Lake: recipes for Seattle's favorite park / Susan Banks and Carol Orr.
    p. cm.
  Includes bibliographical references.
  ISBN 0-87422-235-4 (alk. paper)
   1. Cookery, American. I. Orr, Carol, 1949- II. Title.

TX715 .B215 2000
641.5973—dc21   00-048407

Table of Contents

Acknowledgements ix

Foreword xi

Introduction xiii

Packing for Picnics xv

Map of Green Lake Park xvi

History of Green Lake 1

Chapter 1—Runner's Brunch 9
    Sprinter's Citrus Sippers 11
    Tortilla Torta 12
    Salsa Fresca 13
    Pecan Pumpkin Muffins 14
    Jicama Sticks 15

Chapter 2—Gather on the Greens 17
    Picnic Pâté 19
    Country Greens Salad 20
    Putter's Potato Salad 21
    Lemon Gems 22
    Raspberry Mint Tea 23

Chapter 3—Bathhouse Cocktail Party 25
    Oshi Zushi (Sushi in a Pan) 27
    Japanese Chicken Rounds 29
    Banquet Mushrooms 31
    Tsukune (Japanese Meatballs) 32
    Winter Fruit Platter 34

Chapter 4—Evans Pool Swimmer's Dinner 37
Planning a Pizza Party 39
Party Pizza Dough 40
No-cook Tomato Sauce 41
Spicy Flatbread Sticks 42
Spinach Salad with Warm Garlic Dressing 43
Biscotti with Mascarpone Cream and Strawberries 44

Chapter 5—Seafair Milk Carton Derby Picnic 47
Avocado Mousse 49
Nopales Corn Salsa 50
Captain's Couscous Salad 51
Derby Turkey Empanadas 52
Fresh Fruit Kebabs with Creamy Dip 54

Chapter 6—Children's Paddleboat Party 57
Garden Herb Dip 59
Little Devil Sandwiches 60
Racer's Rotini Salad 61
Five-Spice Fruit Medley 62
Crazy Pizza Cookie 63
Berry Good Lemonade 64

Chapter 7—Pathway of Lights Luminarias Dinner 67
Champagne Mustard Soup 69
Christmas Crackers 70
Minty Grilled Lamb Kebabs 71
Rosemary Walnut Rice 72
Tangy Carrot Coins 73
Raspberry Almond Crisp 74

Chapter 8—Breakfast Before the Regatta 77
Northwest Oven Omelets 79
Good Morning Scones 80
Artichoke and Onion Potatoes 82
Crewman's Fruit Cup 83

Chapter 9—Nature Walk Picnic 85
    Red Pepper Soup 87
    Tabouleh Salad with Feta 88
    Northern White Bean Spread 89
    Roasted Garlic Pita Chips 90
    Nature Date Bars 91
    Naughty Nature Date Bars 92
    Meditation Tea 93

Chapter 10—"Give Back to Green Lake" Buffet.................... 95
    Tomatillo Salsa 97
    Parmesan Tortilla Triangles 98
    Southwestern Caesar Salad 99
    Stick to Your Ribs 100
    Tropical Fruit and Beans............................ 101
    Lemon Heaven Ice with Berries 102

Neighborhood Attractions: A Sampler 105

Selected Bibliography 109

Author Biographies 111

For our husbands,
Stewart and David
and
In Memory of Mildred

Acknowledgements

WRITING A COOKBOOK, we discovered, is a little like raising a child. It's more difficult than can be anticipated, everyone has an opinion, and the outcome is uncertain. With the publication of *Good Times at Green Lake*, our child has finally graduated, and with only a few extra pounds. We relied on our families and friends who graciously tasted and tested. Our sincere thanks to our husbands, Stewart and David, Carol's children, Tammy and Crystal, my mother Virginia, and siblings Scott, Jean, and Ken Banks. Also to our friends Denise Thomas, Carol Ivan, Dana Stabenow, and Julie Newnam who supported and encouraged us in many ways.

We spent numerous hours searching the archives at the Green Lake Library, Seattle Public Library, the City Municipal Archives, Seattle Parks and Recreation, University of Washington Special Collections, and the Museum of History and Industry. Many thanks to the courteous and efficient staff members who assisted us. We also thank Dr. Val Hillers, Department of Food Science and Human Nutrition at Washington State University, for checking the safety of our recipes, and most of all, the WSU Press for their faith in our project.

Foreword

*G*ood Times at Green Lake is a celebration of Green Lake Park and its history. Not only is the lake the hub of the neighborhood, but people from the suburbs of Seattle flock here to run, picnic, and participate in special events. Within the span of a few blocks, you can go on a bird walk, learn to throw pottery, walk to the library, dine at ethnic restaurants, participate in theater, watch world-class boat races, and play tennis. The park is a source of spiritual rejuvenation. People meditate with fishing pole in hand, daydream on the banks, and repose on benches, hands clasped behind their heads.

The idea for *Good Times* evolved from the seasonal activities at the lake: dinner with friends after the Pathway of Lights; a picnic lunch at the Milk Carton Derby Races; breakfast before the regatta. The recipes reflect our love of ethnic foods and the cultural diversity embraced by the community. From Mexican to Mediterranean, they are a blending of cuisines. Each chapter includes a complete menu, but there are no rules. We encourage you to interchange recipes, add some of your own, use prepared ingredients when you're in a hurry, and substitute when necessary.

At a time when adults work through lunch and children practice soccer during dinner, we need to decompress. Good food fosters relaxation and conversation. Moments we carve out of our hectic lives for loved ones become memories. We hope yours are many and lasting.

—Susan Banks and Carol Orr

Introduction

I REMEMBER THE FIRST TIME I met Carol in Anchorage, Alaska, during the 1970s. Just the top of her head was visible as she stirred a stockpot nearly as tall as she was, fingers of steam curling around her. Already a partner in a successful catering business, Carol had inherited the cooking gene—if there is such a thing—from her mother, Mildred, a self-taught cook who baked crusty loaves of bread every week without a measuring cup or KitchenAid.

Though I lacked cooking experience, Carol's partner, Joyce, hired me as an assistant while I was a struggling college student. I watched in awe as their fingers flew, transforming party trays into works of art. Their influence was enduring, prompting me in 1993 to attend Le Cordon Bleu in London. That summer of formal culinary training provided me with the basic skills and foundations for creating recipes.

We have derived our greatest culinary inspiration from our travel experiences, beginning in 1979 when Carol dreamed of going to South America and invited me to accompany her. Despite the revolution occurring in Nicaragua, we headed south. Foods from Central and South America were still uncommon in the United States. We relished plantains grilled over a fire and soup sprinkled with something that looked like parsley, which we later learned was cilantro. At our hotel in Venezuela, the strong, full-bodied coffee cured us of jet lag—long before Starbucks opened at Green Lake! Carol and I have continued to travel together—our latest expedition to the Chianti Wine Festival in Tuscany, Italy—but no other trip has been as dangerous or as memorable as our first. The foods and flavors we were introduced to—simple and earthy—left a lasting impression and have influenced many of our recipes in *Good Times*.

When we lived in Alaska, we enjoyed trips to the lower 48, a necessity to break the tedium of long, dark winters. The beauty of Seattle and the mild temperatures enticed us to relocate. Pike Place Market, a food lover's paradise, confirmed that decision.

After my husband and I moved to Green Lake in 1992, I met neighbors who had been longtime residents. They reminisced about fireworks they had watched from the stoops of their homes and the antics of the Aqua Follies. I began to wonder who had lived in the grand Victorian homes that overlook the lake. When was the railroad trestle near the lawn bowling clubhouse built? What was it like to ride the trolley from downtown Seattle to the lake? As my interest in the Green Lake neighborhood grew, I became obsessed with uncovering its history—from the birth of the lake to the building of the Bathhouse Theatre. Every landmark at the park has a story; we feature several of them in our ten chapter vignettes.

May *Good Times at Green Lake* inspire you to explore the lake, learn about its colorful history, and share in a food adventure with friends!

Packing for Picnics

When packing for a picnic, it's important to observe the following food safety guidelines:

- Use only an insulated cooler, with plenty of ice or gel packs. Blocks of ice don't melt as quickly as cubes (inexpensive blocks can be made by freezing water in milk containers).

- Take hot and cold drinks in insulated thermoses.

- Prepare foods as close to the time you leave as possible, except those that need to be chilled before packing in a cooler.

- Immediately refrigerate cooked foods that are to be transported cold.

- Pack the most vulnerable foods—meats, dairy products, seafood, and eggs—in the coldest section of the cooler.

- Keep hot foods 140°F or above and cold foods 45°F or below. The danger zone for food is 45° to 140°F. Food is safe at this range for a *maximum* of two cumulative hours.

- Pack hot and cold foods separately.

- Take only the amount of food you plan to eat.

- Travel with your cooler in the car rather than in the trunk on warm days. When you arrive at your destination, place it in the shade.

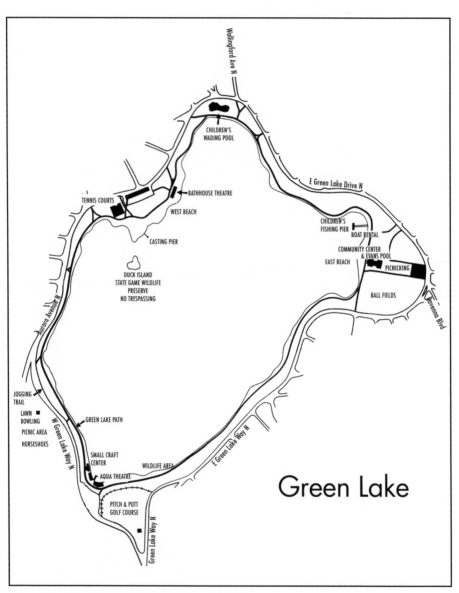

Map courtesy of Seattle Department of Parks and Recreation.

History of Green Lake

SEATTLE'S FAVORITE PARK, Green Lake, bears little resemblance to its humble beginnings as a mosquito-infested swamp. On a sunny day, the sweet scent of coconut oil wafts from sunbathers, while rollerbladers and runners race around the pathway. Green Lake's reputation for being the most popular park in the city is well earned. At the height of summer, as many as 40,000 tourists and residents visit the lake during a one-week period. Some walk dogs almost as tall as they are, while others relax on canvas stools, fishing pole in hand, waiting for a nibble. Nearby, readers of all ages browse at the Green Lake Library, one of Seattle's first Carnegie-funded branches, now on the National Register of Historic Places. Special festivities throughout the year, including the Seafair Milk Carton Derby, have become family affairs.

Over the years, a variety of events have drawn people to the lake: model powerboat races, flattie regattas, cross country track meets, water ski carnivals, fly casting tournaments, a Huckleberry Finn look-alike contest, and a blind fishing derby, among others. The Fourth of July fireworks display was a favorite celebration. Long-time Green Lake residents reminisce about watching them from the stoops of their homes. Many events were moved to other venues after residents complained about noise and congestion. Powerboat races once billed as a "$2000 event" have long been banned; 1984 was the last year for the Seafair limited hydroplane races. The Bite of Seattle attracted so many food lovers that it was moved to the Seattle Center.

The popularity of Green Lake has been the source of many of its woes. At times the park has battled with problems brought about by urbanization. There have often been financial struggles as well, yet local commitment to preserving the park has remained strong.

Contrary to popular belief, the lake is not manmade. It is the offspring of the Vashon Glacial Sheet that covered Puget Sound some 50,000 years ago. The runoff from the melting glacier formed Lake Russell, which stretched from Everett to Olympia. Eventually this large lake disappeared, leaving as its remnant the three lakes in the north end of Seattle: Green, Haller, and Bitter lakes. Green Lake, which is naturally shallow and nutrient-rich, was plagued with algae from the beginning. Hence its unflattering name.

In 1869, after forging his way through the woods and canoeing across the water, the first white settler, Erhart Seifried, stepped onto the shores of Green Lake. Soon after building a cabin on the northwest shore, "Green Lake John," as he came to be known, fell in love. But the woman he wooed wouldn't have him until he owned a cow. Unable to afford one, the chagrined settler approached his boss who sympathetically advanced him the money. After the wedding, the happy groom built another cabin to house milk and vegetables.

Cabins on the property once owned by "Green Lake John," the first white settler who homesteaded at Green Lake in 1869. *MSCUA, Univ. of Washington Libraries, Neg. UW 593*

In 1887, the property was sold to real estate investor William D. Wood who platted the land. Four years later, in order to make the area more accessible, Wood partnered with developer Edward C. Kilbourne to form the Green Lake Electric Railway Company. The area boomed during the early 1890s. A. L. Parker built a sawmill where the community center and playfield now stand and linked it with a logging railroad to Fremont. A ten-acre amusement park, about which little is known, was built in what is now west Green Lake. Guy Phinney arrived in 1889 and bought 188 acres of land southwest of the lake on which he built a small zoo, a conservatory, flower gardens, picnic grounds, a playfield, and boathouse. He allowed the public to use the park, but with one stipulation that probably

The F. A. McDonald home, built in 1890 at the south end of Green Lake. At the lower left is a trolley car of the Green Lake Electric Railway Co. *MSCUA, Univ. of Washington Libraries, La Roche 61.*

irked some visitors: he banned dogs from the property. He even posted a sign threatening to shoot them! Nevertheless, people rode the trolley line from downtown to the lake to enjoy the amenities. In the year 1900, nine years after Green Lake was annexed to Seattle, Phinney's park was sold to the city for $100,000—despite protests that it was too far from downtown. Today, it is the site of Woodland Park Zoo.

At the time of the sale, about 1500 people were calling Green Lake home. Before long, most of the forest, except for Phinney's land, had been replaced with houses. Businesses sprang up, including a general merchandise and feed store, blacksmith shop, dry goods store, and a hotel. The area continued to grow. In 1905 the lake was given by the state of Washington to the city for a park. Soon afterwards, the Green Lake Improvement Club was formed, the first of many organizations to support the park. One of their first projects was to press the Seattle City Council into building wooden sidewalks. Usage of the lake, though, was limited. The only land around it was a narrow strip squeezed between the water and the streetcar line. To increase the acreage, the Olmsted brothers, designers of Green Lake Park and numerous others in Seattle, recommended reducing the water level of the lake. In 1911, the city adopted the Olmsteds' plan and began a twenty-two-year project that lowered the lake by seven feet and added nearly 100 acres of land around it. Unfortunately, the preexisting algae problem was made worse because the natural springs and creeks which had fed into the lake were cut off, causing stagnation.

Green Lake, about 1904. *MSCUA, Univ. of Washington Libraries, Neg. UW 14542*

Nevertheless, Green Lake remained popular and improvements continued. Construction of a bathhouse on the west shore began in 1927. The following year it opened with large changing rooms for bathers, a first aid station, and boat storage. In 1970, when evolving social code deemed it acceptable to wear bathing suits to the lake, the changing rooms were remodeled into a 130-seat theatre, appropriately named the Bathhouse Theatre. Although often earning accolades for its productions, the company was frequently in the red. The limited number of seats and other setbacks eventually overwhelmed the theatre; in January 1999 it closed its doors. The following year, the city selected the Seattle Public Theatre as the new resident company.

In 1929 one year after the original bathhouse was completed, the fieldhouse—now the Green Lake Community Center—was constructed. Funded by a $105,000 bond, the *Seattle Washington Star* billed it as the "Greatest West of the Mississippi." Though the main attraction was its gymnasium, the building also had showers and meeting rooms.

In 1936 an ambitious project to dredge the lake in order to alleviate the algae problem was funded by the Works Progress Administration (WPA). In all, Seattle received $2.2 million dollars from the WPA to enhance its parks and create jobs for the unemployed. In addition to dredging Green Lake, plans included the construction of an artificial island and a fountain in the middle of the lake. The island was built to provide a nesting area for a pair of swans given to the park by Victoria, British Columbia. Later it was dedicated as a wildlife refuge, the Waldo Waterfowl Sanctuary, popularly known as Duck Island. The other two projects were never completed. An explosion on the dredge and financial problems halted the dredging in 1937. Plans for the fountain were also scrapped. Attempts to resolve the algae problem continued during the '30s, but the stubborn "green plague" persisted.

The Green Lake retail district had its own ups and downs. At times business thrived. After the University and Montlake bridges were built in 1919 and 1926, respectively, business dropped off. There was also a decline after the Northgate Shopping Center was built in 1950. In that same year, however, the notable Aqua Theatre was constructed at Green Lake in a record seventy-five days, in time to open for Seafair. The original structure provided seating for 5200 people overlooking an enormous stage with two diving platforms. The Aqua Follies, Broadway specials, and musicals entertained capacity crowds during the summertime. The highlight was during the World's Fair in the summer of 1962 when Bob Hope, Juliet Prowse, and Jimmie Rodgers packed the theatre.

After the Seattle Center was built, the Aqua Theatre struggled to compete. Fickle weather often hampered the shows. Sadly, 1965 was the last season. In 1979, most of the structure was torn down to make room for

Model sailboat races in 1934. *Seattle PI Collection, Museum of History and Industry*

the boating facilities on the south end. As a tribute to their popularity, the Follies returned to the Aqua Theatre for Seafair's 50th anniversary celebration in 1999.

The fifties brought other new developments to the shores of the lake. The crew program moved to a permanent home in 1950 when the Clarence Massart Boat House was built on the west shore. In 1955, workers poured concrete for the beamless eggshell roof on the Evans Pool, the first of its kind in Seattle.

Plans to improve the lake sometimes divided the community. In 1958, there was heated debate over building a dike to divide the lake into separate swimming and fishing areas. It wasn't the first plan to section the lake. In 1941, the Green Lake Commercial Club proposed making a tropical swim beach by enclosing a portion of the lake and filling it with warm water from a substation. Neither plan was implemented, but everyone agreed that the lake needed to be cleaned up.

In the early 1960s, another massive cleanup was undertaken to remove the algae and muck from the bottom of the lake. Freshwater inlets were also installed, a seawall built, and the beaches were sanded. Still, algae continued to proliferate. In August 1999, health officials once again closed the lake due to the overgrowth of algae. In retrospect, scientists conceded that the problem might not have been worse than previous years. A public forum was held to discuss the issue, and it remains the number one concern of the Green Lake Park Alliance, a volunteer organization.

Overpopulation of Canada geese continues to be a problem at Green Lake Park.
Susan Banks

Other than the water quality issue, nothing has caused more disputes than the congestion of the inner pathway. Bikers, runners, walkers, and rollerbladers jostle one another, sometimes colliding with disastrous results. Over the years, residents and officials have presented a variety of plans to relieve the congestion. Some, including a proposal to ban wheels or restrict their use during peak hours, sparked angry debate. The controversy heated up in May 1992 when a pregnant walker was hit by a youth on a bicycle, and spent five days in the hospital. In 1995 a plan was finally agreed upon; the city council approved $2.6 million for renovation of the inner pathway, including a crushed gravel path and a 13½-foot-wide asphalt lane.

Green Lake continues to evolve and wrestle with the problems it has encountered since the first boom. The shallow lake carved from the belly of a glacier has been diked, dredged, filled, lowered, sanded, stocked, and chemically treated. Water quality remains a primary concern despite all the efforts. Eurasian milfoil still chokes the water if left alone, Canada geese droppings litter the beaches, and swimmers may later find themselves scratching. Like the ecosystem, societal balance is often delicate. Residents in the retail district would prefer not to be neighbors with Vitamilk Dairy, located in the heart of the community since 1940, but the company has no plans to move. The pathway, though wide and smooth since the renovation, is a freeway of people on a sunny day—like I-5 to the east.

Despite the issues, the charm of Green Lake outweighs its challenges. Concerned residents work together to keep the park and the neighborhood healthy. An active Community Council provides a forum for discussing and planning for the future. The Green Lake Park Alliance sponsors landscape enhancement and educational programs. A task force called Green Lake 2020 is making long-term recommendations on issues concerning zoning and density.

Green Lake Park offers a gathering place for the community, as well as a scenic location for enjoying nature and exercise. Couples pushing strollers, senior citizens from the Hearthstone Retirement Center, and people in wheelchairs all share the 342-acre park. Diehard runners meet in the early morning hours to exercise before going to work. Anglers fish for trout stocked by the Department of Parks and Recreation. Occasionally in winter the lake freezes and residents dust off their ice skates to take a spin. Athletes and spectators alike enjoy lawn bowling, golf, tennis, canoeing, volleyball, baseball and other sports that abound in the park. Green Lake, jewel of Seattle, is a park for all people.

Green Lake Marathon held in 1961. *Seattle PI Collection, Museum of History and Industry*

Chapter 1

Runner's Brunch

RUNNING AROUND GREEN LAKE is relaxing, especially in the fall. Leaves the size of hands crunch underfoot while the chilly air refreshes the skin like peppermint. Every day exercise buffs don their shoes and pound the 2.8-mile inner pathway. Even President Clinton jogged around Green Lake during his visit to Seattle in 1993. Two stretching stations with diagrams for exercises were installed in 1982. They're located behind the Aqua Theatre on the southwest shore and near the boat rental on the northeast end. Occasionally Green Lake hosts a race. Check *Northwest Runner* magazine or inquire at the Super Jock 'N Jill store located at 7210 East Green Lake Drive North.

In the peak of summer, as many as 7,000 people a day visit the lake. To accommodate the heavy usage, the pathway was paved with asphalt in the early 1970s. Gradually it deteriorated to the point of being dangerous, particularly for the disabled. Tree roots caused the path to buckle and, in some places, low spots filled with water. The biggest problem continued to be overcrowding, particularly on sunny days. Accidents occurred as bikers, joggers, and rollerbladers all jockeyed for space. In 1992 a drive to ban bikes and rollerblades failed. Short-term solutions—posting more signs, repainting the centerline, and clarifying the courtesy code—proved inadequate.

Several years passed before the city agreed on a plan that met the goals of the project: to accommodate all park users, minimize tree removal, and to build a path with the natural look of an urban park. In November 1995, the city of Seattle approved a plan and the funds to renovate the path. The final bill came to $2.6 million, almost a million dollars a mile. The project was finished in 1997, complete with a 5½-foot-wide crushed granite pedestrian trail and a 13½-foot-wide asphalt lane. Costly underground improvements included drainage pipes, a thicker foundation, and root barriers.

Carol and I confess that we're not runners. We're content to stroll the pathway contemplating the world, solving problems, and daydreaming about our next dinner party. The changing seasons ensure a view that is never the same. In the springtime, we look for fuzzy ducklings hugging the shoreline and year-round there is plenty of good people- and dog-watching.

For brunch, we prefer lighter fare with robust flavor. The *Tortilla Torta* is an unusual alternative to the traditional quiche. Begin your meal with *Sprinter's Citrus Sippers*, a refreshing cool-down drink. In the meantime, you can quickly assemble this south-of-the-border brunch. Make the *Tortilla Torta* ahead of time and rewarm it before serving.

Sprinter's Citrus Sippers

Good with a splash of rum or tequila.

1 can (12 ounces) frozen limeade concentrate
3½ cups cold water
1 cup fresh grapefruit juice (2 or 3 small pink grapefruit)
⅛ teaspoon Tabasco, or to taste
Coarse salt for the rim of the glasses (optional)
1 lime, cut into wedges

Put the limeade in a large pitcher. Add the water and grapefruit juice; stir well. Add the Tabasco and stir again. Dip the rim of the serving glasses in the limeade mixture and then the salt. Serve the Sippers over crushed ice. Float a wedge of lime in each glass.

Yields 6 servings

Tortilla Torta

A Southwest alternative to quiche.

6 10-inch flour tortillas
6 eggs
2 tablespoons flour
½ cup buttermilk
2 cups (about 8 ounces) grated pepper jack cheese
3 green onions, sliced (optional)
4 ounces roasted red peppers, drained and chopped
½ teaspoon salt
¼ teaspoon pepper
1 tablespoon butter, melted
9 x 3-inch springform pan

1. Preheat the oven to 375 degrees. Spray the springform pan lightly with vegetable oil. Line it with 5 of the tortillas, overlapping them and gently pressing them against the sides of the pan. (Be careful not to tear them.) You may have to pleat them in some places. Extend the tortillas about 2 inches above the rim. Set aside.

2. Whisk the eggs in a large bowl. Add the flour, buttermilk, cheese, green onions, red peppers, salt, and pepper; stir well. Pour the filling into the tortilla shell. Gently bend the edges of the tortillas over the filling. With scissors or a knife, trim the remaining tortilla so it will fit on top. Brush the edges with water. Brush the tops of the tortillas in the pan with water. Put the tortilla on top and gently press. Brush melted butter on top.

3. Bake about 1 hour, checking it after 15 minutes for browning. Cover the top with foil after it has browned. To check for doneness, make a small slit in the top and press gently. If the egg is runny, continue baking. Remove the torta from the oven and let stand 20 minutes. Release the springform. Place the torta on a serving platter. Serve with Salsa Fresca and sour cream.

Yields 6 servings

Salsa Fresca

Use a serrano chili if you like hot foods. You can also add more garlic.

4 plum tomatoes, seeded and coarsely chopped (about 2 cups)
1 shallot, peeled and chopped
1 fresh jalapeño chili pepper, finely chopped
2 cloves garlic, chopped
1 teaspoon olive oil
3 tablespoons roughly chopped cilantro
Freshly squeezed lemon or lime juice to taste

Combine the ingredients in a small bowl. Add coarse salt and freshly ground pepper to taste. Let stand at room temperature for one hour. Serve with the Tortilla Torta.

Yields about 2 cups

Pecan Pumpkin Muffins

These wholesome muffins have a subtle sweetness that complements the Southwest flavors in this menu.

2 cups flour
½ cup packed brown sugar
½ cup pecans, coarsely chopped plus 12 pecan halves (for the muffin tops)
2 teaspoons baking powder
1 teaspoon ground cinnamon
¼ teaspoon ground ginger
⅛ teaspoon ground cloves
½ teaspoon salt
½ cup olive oil
1 cup canned pumpkin
¼ cup milk
2 eggs, room temperature

1. Preheat the oven to 400 degrees. Lightly spray a muffin pan with oil. In a large bowl, combine the flour, brown sugar, ½ cup pecans, baking powder, cinnamon, ginger, cloves and salt. Make a well in the center.

2. Whisk the olive oil, pumpkin, milk, and eggs in a medium bowl. Pour into the well of the dry ingredients. Stir until just mixed. Fill the muffin tins almost to the top. Place one pecan-half on the center of each muffin, pressing it down about halfway into the batter. Bake 20 minutes, or until a toothpick inserted comes out clean. Let stand 5 minutes before removing from the pan. Serve immediately, or cool and cover tightly. Serve with whipped butter.

Yields 12 muffins

Jicama Sticks

Jicama is commonly used in Mexican cooking. This slightly sweet vegetable can be served raw or cooked. Try it in salads to give them a crunch.

1 jicama (about 2 pounds)
1 cup orange juice
½ medium onion, chopped
¼ teaspoon salt
⅛ teaspoon ground cumin
Chili powder for garnish

1. Use a knife to remove the skin from the jicama. Slice it into sticks about ½ x ½-inch wide. Combine the orange juice, onion, salt, and cumin in a small bowl. Lay the jicama sticks in a single layer in a rectangular baking dish. Pour the orange juice mixture over them.

2. Marinate in the refrigerator 2 to 4 hours, turning the sticks occasionally. Drain and discard the marinade. Season the jicama sticks lightly with salt; dust with chili powder. Place several sticks on each guest's plate, or arrange them on a serving platter in a spiral pattern.

Yields about 20 sticks

Roy G. Knudson, lawn bowling at the Woodland Park Lawn Bowling Club, watched by Mickey Roberts (behind) and Chet Madden (seated). *Courtesy of the Woodlawn Park Lawn Bowling Club.*

Chapter 2

Gather on the Greens
Lawn Bowling and Pitch and Putt

O N THE SOUTH SHORE of the lake near the Aqua Theatre, people of all ages can enjoy outdoor activities. One of those activities, lawn bowling, is an ancient and dignified sport, similar to bocce. The object—to roll your balls (called bowls) closest to a small white ball (jack)—is harder than it appears. The bowls are not perfectly spherical and are heavier on one side. Modern ones weigh about three pounds and are made of plastic. Other variables, particularly the weather and condition of the playing surface, also affect the game.

The Woodland Park Lawn Bowling Club is located between Aurora Avenue North and the southwest corner of Green Lake. Follow the road behind the Aqua Theatre past the tennis courts and up the hill. On the left, resembling a stone wall, is the remains of a railroad trestle. Just ahead, nestled on a hill above the lake, is the clubhouse, rebuilt in 1996 after an arson fire. Old timers reminisce about the trophy cabinet that was destroyed and, if asked, will show you the remains of a wooden bowl, charred but still recognizable.

Discussion of building a bowling green began in the late 1920s, with park board members finally committing to it in 1931. When the greens first opened a couple years later, the City Recreation Department operated them, charging 25 cents per game. In the early 1930s, the Woodland Park Lawn Bowling Club formed, and by 1935 was running the greens. Today, Seattle Parks and Recreation maintains the greens with help from club members.

Players can bowl year-round, except during freezing weather when damage to the lawn may occur. Though Woodland Park Lawn Bowling Club is private, visitors are welcome, and free classes are offered each spring by members eager to teach their sport. Initially, bowls can be borrowed, but enthusiasts who pursue the sport must buy their own and pay an annual membership fee to join the club.

Lawn bowling can be played in singles, pairs, triples, or rinks (four players on a team). During the course of an average game, players walk about a mile. Flat-soled shoes are required in order to protect the greens. Street clothes are permitted, but "whites" are still traditional for tournaments. Horseshoe pits and picnic tables are located near the upper green. The phone number for the clubhouse is 206-782-1515.

If golf is the game of choice, head east from the Woodland Park Lawn Bowling club to Pitch and Putt, a nine-hole public golf course. In 1948, Miss Gloria Hemrich signed a lease for seven acres of parkland and constructed the course. Miss Hemrich operated it for about five years before selling it to the city for $8200. Well suited for families, Pitch and Putt helped relieve long lines at regular city golf courses. Pitch and Putt is located at 5701 West Green Lake Way North, and open 9 a.m. until dusk, spring through fall. The telephone number is 206-632-2280. Reservations are not required.

After you've had your fill of the "greens," enjoy a leisurely picnic at the tables by the horseshoe pits. Some of our most memorable meals in Italy were simple ones eaten alfresco; we continue the tradition with this menu. Earthy Mediterranean flavors—garlic, lemon, and oregano—complement outdoor entertaining. *Picnic Pâté,* a savory, layered meatloaf, is easy to make. *Iced Raspberry Mint Tea* and *Lemon Gems* finish the meal with just a touch of sweetness.

Picnic Pâté

This meatloaf is showy, but easy to prepare. For best results, make the day before serving.

¾ pound lean ground beef
¾ pound Italian bulk pork sausage
½ medium onion, coarsely chopped
3 large cloves garlic, chopped
3 tablespoons chopped fresh basil, or 2 teaspoons dried
1 tablespoon dried oregano
½ teaspoon freshly ground pepper
½ cup tomato juice
½ cup dried fine bread crumbs
1 egg
4 ounces prosciutto or thinly sliced ham, preferably Black Forest
4 ounces feta cheese, crumbled
6 ounces roasted red peppers, drained, chopped, and patted dry

1. Preheat the oven to 350 degrees. In a large bowl thoroughly mix the meat, onion, garlic, basil, oregano, pepper, tomato juice, bread crumbs, and egg. Divide the mixture into thirds.

2. Put ⅓ of the meat into a 8½ x 4½ x 2½-inch loaf pan and spread evenly. Layer the ham evenly over the meat. (Use another third of the meat mixture for the next **two** layers.) Cover ham with a thin layer of the meat mixture. Layer the cheese evenly over the meat. Top with another thin layer of the meat mixture. Place the red peppers evenly over the meat. Spread the remaining third of the meat mixture over the peppers.

3. Bake an hour, or until firm. (It should register at least 160° on a meat thermometer.) Drain and leave in the pan; chill in the refrigerator 4 hours. Cover tightly and pack in a cooler; keep chilled. Invert on plate and cut into thick slices. When we serve this at home, we prefer it at room temperature.

Yields 6 to 8 servings

Country Greens Salad

Toast the nuts ahead of time. Put the dressing in a small jar and give it a good shake before you dress the salad.

12 cups small mixed salad greens, washed and dried
1 can (11 ounces) mandarin oranges, drained and dried

TOASTED WALNUTS
½ tablespoon butter
½ cup walnut halves
1 teaspoon sugar
¼ teaspoon ground cinnamon
Generous pinch of cayenne, or to taste
Pinch of salt

DRESSING
2 tablespoons balsamic vinegar
1 tablespoon raspberry or strawberry jam
1 tablespoon chopped shallots
Dash of red pepper flakes
⅛ teaspoon freshly ground pepper
½ cup vegetable oil

1. To make toasted walnuts: melt the butter in a small saucepan over medium-low heat. Add the walnuts, sugar, cinnamon, cayenne, and salt. Mix well with a wooden spoon. Toast the nuts until browned (watch closely), stirring occasionally. Remove from the heat; cool. Put in a small container.

2. To make dressing: combine the balsamic vinegar, jam, shallots, red pepper flakes, and pepper in a small bowl. Gradually whisk in the oil. Add salt to taste. Put in a leakproof container or jar, and pack in a cooler.

3. Put the salad greens and mandarin oranges in separate containers; pack in a cooler. Keep chilled. To assemble: put the salad greens in a large bowl. Add the walnuts and mandarin oranges. Dress the salad.

Yields 6 servings

Putter's Potato Salad

Savor the Greek flavors of this nontraditional potato salad.

6 small to medium white potatoes (about 2 pounds), peeled
½ red onion, thinly sliced
¾ cup Greek olives, pitted and cut in half
¾ cup (about 3 ounces) grated kasseri cheese, or good quality Parmesan
1½ teaspoons chopped fresh marjoram, or ½ teaspoon dried
1½ tablespoons chopped fresh dill, or 1 teaspoon dried

DRESSING
3 tablespoons white wine vinegar
1 tablespoon fresh lemon juice
2 cloves garlic, chopped
1 teaspoon sugar
½ teaspoon salt
¼ teaspoon freshly ground pepper
½ cup extra virgin olive oil

1. Boil or steam the potatoes in salted water until just tender. Meanwhile, prepare the dressing. Combine the vinegar, lemon juice, garlic, sugar, salt and pepper in a small bowl. Gradually whisk in the olive oil.

2. Drain the potatoes and cool just enough to handle; cut into slices about ¼-inch thick. Put in a large bowl. Pour the dressing over the potatoes and stir carefully, until well coated. Add the onion, olives, cheese, marjoram, and dill; stir carefully. Put in a covered container and chill in the refrigerator; pack in a cooler. When we serve this at home, we prefer it at room temperature.

Yields 6 servings

Lemon Gems

Serve these cookies with fresh fruit.

1 stick (½ cup) unsalted butter, softened
5 teaspoons fresh lemon juice
½ teaspoon vanilla
1 teaspoon finely grated lemon zest
2 cups cake (soft pastry) flour
¾ cup plus ½ cup powdered sugar
½ cup sweetened, shredded or flaked coconut
⅛ teaspoon salt

1. Preheat the oven to 300 degrees. Put the butter in a medium bowl and beat it with a wooden spoon until very soft. Add the lemon juice, vanilla, lemon zest, flour, the ¾ cup of powdered sugar, coconut, and salt. Mix well until the dough is crumbly and turns slightly yellow. Use your hands to form the dough into a smooth ball.

2. Lightly oil a baking sheet. Form the dough into walnut-sized balls. Bake 25 minutes, or until just firm. Remove and place on a wire rack; roll in the remaining powdered sugar while slightly warm. Cool completely before packing in an airtight container.

Yields about 25 cookies

Raspberry Mint Tea

A refreshing tea for a hot day.

6 cups cold water
2 cups fresh or frozen raspberries, thawed
4 teaspoons loose Darjeeling tea, or 4 tea bags
5 teaspoons loose mint tea, or 5 tea bags
10 whole allspice, crushed slightly with the blade of a knife
1 teaspoon vanilla
3 tablespoons honey, or to taste

Bring the water to a boil; remove from the heat. Add the raspberries, tea, and allspice. Steep five minutes. Strain the tea through a fine strainer; add the vanilla and honey; stir well. Serve over ice, or let stand at room temperature 30 minutes and chill. Pour into an insulated thermos.

Yields 6 cups

Green Lake Bathhouse, June 25, 1936. *Seattle Municipal Archives*

Chapter 3

Bathhouse Cocktail Party

WHEN THE SUN SHINES at Green Lake, bare skin and spandex are prevalent. The word "modest" isn't one that comes to mind. Some of my neighbors remember when it was scandalous to wear a bathing suit to the lake. The bathhouse, built in 1927 by a state program for out-of-work-laborers, provided large changing rooms for swimmers. Showers, boat storage and a first aid station were also housed there. Eventually, as societal standards relaxed, people began wearing their bathing suits to the lake and private changing rooms were no longer needed.

In 1970, with funds from the King County Forward Thrust Program, the city remodeled the recreation facility into an intimate lakeside theatre. When money ran out before seating could be purchased, the Ballard Jaycees spearheaded the Bathhouse Theatre Seats Project: a fifty-dollar donation bought a chair with a commemorative plaque on the arm. The project was successful. The theatre opened with adult productions staged September through May; high school performances were held during the summer.

Despite humble beginnings, the Bathhouse Theatre soon received accolades for producing innovative plays. Under Brian Thompson, the first resident director, the company won the Region VI American Community Theatre Association Play Festival in 1971. Two years later, they represented the United States in the Dundalk International Amateur Theatre Festival in Ireland with their production of *The Importance of Being Earnest*.

A new artistic director and theatre company took up residence in the Bathhouse in 1980. Arne Zaslove, cofounder of the University of Washington Professional Actor Training Program, introduced shows based on the European ensemble tradition, using mask, dance and song. The company continued to win critical and popular acclaim for its creative approach to the classics. In a typical season, the theatre hosted five shows, including a Christmas play, Shakespearean productions, and original musical reviews.

In spite of its respectable accomplishments and steady patronage, the theatre, like other small companies, struggled financially. By the late 1990s, the Bathhouse Theatre was in the red for over $400,000. High rent, a limited number of seats, and the cancellation of a European Cabaret (due to pressure from park activists) contributed to the company's mounting debt and ultimate closure in January 1999. After remaining vacant for a year, in February 2000, the city announced it had selected the Seattle Public Theatre to make the Bathhouse its home. The company uses drama to focus on social issues.

A cocktail party is an elegant way to entertain your friends before an evening at the theatre. Asian food takes center stage in this menu created by Carol. In the 1980s she lived in Japan under the guise of teaching English as a second language; her real motive was to study the cuisine. Symbolic, artful, and creative, Asian food shares a rich tradition with the theatre.

Serve toasted rice crackers and roasted nuts for appetizers, and fortune cookies with the *Winter Fruit Platter* at the end of the meal.

Oshi Zushi
(Sushi in a Pan)

Sushi in a pan is easier to make than individual pieces. Experiment with your favorite kinds of seafood.

1¼ cups medium grain rice
1½ cups cold water
¼ teaspoon salt
2 to 3 ounces canned firm seafood, such as smoked oysters, clams, and tiny shrimp
1 sheet nori (dried seaweed), sushi grade
1 teaspoon finely grated orange zest
1 tablespoon chopped cilantro

SEASONED VINEGAR
6 tablespoons rice vinegar
¼ cup sugar
1½ teaspoons salt
1½ teaspoons finely grated fresh ginger

1. To make rice: pour the rice into a medium bowl and rinse with cold water from the tap, stirring it with your hand. When the water turns milky, drain it. Repeat the process several times until the water is clear.

2. Put the rice in a strainer and let stand thirty minutes. Pour the rice into a medium saucepan and cover with the 1½ cups water. Bring to a boil over medium-high heat and add the ¼ teaspoon salt; boil about one minute. Stir a few times. Reduce the heat to low and cover with a tight fitting lid; cook 20 minutes. Remove from the heat and let the rice stand, covered, 10 minutes. (Don't lift the lid.)

3. To make seasoned vinegar: combine the rice vinegar, sugar, salt, and ginger in a small saucepan. Warm (but don't boil), until the sugar and salt dissolve; cool to room temperature. Pour the seasoned vinegar over the seafood. Let stand 5 minutes. Drain and reserve the vinegar; fold

the vinegar into the hot rice a little at a time. (Add just enough so the rice is moist but not mushy.) Lightly oil an 8 x 8-inch noncorrosive pan and spread half the rice evenly over the bottom. Cover with the nori and press firmly. Add the remaining rice and spread evenly; press firmly.

4. Arrange the seafood (slice large pieces) randomly over the surface, pressing it into the rice. Sprinkle the orange zest and cilantro on top; press firmly. Cover tightly and chill 4 hours. Cut into 16 squares and carefully remove from the pan with a spatula. Serve with wasabi (Japanese horseradish) and soy sauce.

Yields 16 squares

Japanese Chicken Rounds

When these chicken rounds are sliced, their colorful centers look like flowers.

MARINADE
½ cup mirin* or sweet white wine
½ cup low-sodium soy sauce
¼ cup sugar
4 cloves garlic, finely chopped
2 tablespoons finely grated fresh ginger
1 tablespoon fresh lemon juice
Pinch of salt and pepper

2 boneless skinless chicken breasts (4 halves)
8 thin fresh string beans
1 medium carrot, peeled and cut into 5-inch strips a little thicker than matchsticks
2 or 3 green onions, cut into 5-inch strips
½ medium red pepper, cut into thin strips

1. Preheat the oven to 350 degrees. To make marinade: combine the mirin, soy sauce, sugar, garlic, ginger, lemon juice, salt, and pepper in a small glass bowl. Whisk until well blended; set aside.

2. Cut the chicken breasts in half and trim the fat. Remove the tenderloin from underneath and use another time for stir fry. Place each breast between plastic wrap and pound lightly on the underside until as thin as possible without tearing. Trim the ragged edges.

3. Place a couple pieces of each vegetable widthwise near the narrowest end of each chicken breast. Roll tightly into a log shape, trimming the ends of the vegetables if necessary. Secure the chicken roll with wooden toothpicks and place in a baking dish, seam side down.

---

*Sweet cooking rice wine available in the Asian section of most supermarkets.

4. Pour the marinade over the chicken and cover with foil; bake 35 minutes, or until juices run clear and the chicken is springy to the touch.

5. Remove from the oven; strain the marinade and reserve it. Let the chicken stand until cool enough to handle. Carefully remove the toothpicks. If you prefer to serve it cold, cover and chill in the refrigerator 2 hours. Slice each roll into ½-inch rounds with a serrated knife. Serve with the marinade on the side.

Yields about 20 rounds

Banquet Mushrooms

Even people who don't like tofu will enjoy these mushrooms.

½ cup crumbled soft tofu, drained and patted dry
¼ cup walnuts, chopped
½ cup fine dried bread crumbs
2 tablespoons chopped green onions
1 medium clove garlic, minced
½ teaspoon minced fresh ginger
2 tablespoons prepared hoisin sauce
½ cup mandarin oranges, drained and coarsely chopped
1 egg white
18 mushrooms (about 2 inches in diameter), washed and stemmed
1 tablespoon unsalted butter, melted

1. Preheat the oven to 375 degrees. In a small bowl combine the tofu, walnuts, bread crumbs, green onions, garlic, ginger, hoisin sauce, mandarin oranges, and egg white. Brush the mushroom caps with a little butter. Mound the filling into caps. Save stems for another recipe.

2. Place the mushrooms on a baking sheet. Bake 12 minutes, or until the tops are lightly browned. Remove and serve immediately.

Yields 18 appetizers

Tsukune
(Japanese Meatballs)

These meatballs are lighter than traditional ones. The dashi soup stock balances the sweetness of the maple syrup.

MEATBALLS
½ pound ground chicken
¼ cup finely chopped onion
¼ cup finely grated carrot
½ cup fine dried bread crumbs
1 egg, lightly beaten
2 cloves garlic, finely chopped
1 teaspoon finely grated fresh ginger
¼ teaspoon salt
⅛ teaspoon pepper

SAUCE
1 tablespoon cornstarch
½ teaspoon dashi flakes* dissolved in 1 cup hot water
2 tablespoons mirin**
⅓ cup low-sodium soy sauce
¼ cup maple syrup
Toasted sesame seeds for garnish

1. To make meatballs: preheat the oven to 350 degrees; lightly oil a baking sheet. Combine the chicken, onion, carrots, bread crumbs, egg, garlic, ginger, salt, and pepper in a medium bowl; mix well. Form the mixture into balls about 1½ inches in diameter. Bake 15 to 20 minutes, or until lightly browned, turning once.

2. To make sauce: dissolve the cornstarch in about 2 teaspoons cold water. Combine the dashi stock, mirin, soy sauce, and maple syrup in a medium

---

*Soup stock available in the Asian section of most supermarkets.
**Sweet cooking rice wine available in the Asian section of most supermarkets.

saucepan over medium-high heat; bring to a boil. Whisk the cornstarch into the sauce and return it to a boil. Reduce the heat and gently add the meatballs. Simmer 10 minutes, or until the sauce thickens and coats the back of a spoon. Remove from heat. Serve in a chafing dish, or arrange on a deep platter; sprinkle with toasted sesame seeds.

Yields about 18 meatballs

Winter Fruit Platter

Asian dinners often end with a fruit platter rather than sweets. In Japan, fruit carving is an art, and sometimes only one may be served. Summer fruits are plentiful, but in winter the choices are fewer. The following fruits can usually be found during the colder months and, when cut into different shapes, make a beautiful presentation. Choose fragrant, unblemished fruit and cut it into wedges, segments, cubes, slices, and spears. Other available fresh fruits, such as melons, cherries, plums, grapes, or oranges, can be used to complete the platter. Substitute good quality canned fruit as necessary.

ASIAN PEARS
These are crunchy and slightly sweet. Choose pears that are fragrant and store in the refrigerator. Peel and cut into thin rounds to expose the pretty, flower-like core. Dip in acidulated water (a little lemon juice mixed with water) to keep them from turning brown. If unavailable, use other varieties of pears.

CARAMBOLA (star fruit)
The flavor of this small fruit ranges from sweet to sour. When sliced cross-wise, the slices look like stars. Trim brown edges.

KIWI
Choose firm fruit and use when slightly soft. Peel the thin brown skin; slice or cut into wedges. Refrigerate when ripe.

PAPAYA
This fruit has a sweet floral flavor. Look for papaya that is partially or completely yellow, and gives a little. Chill, cut in half lengthwise, scoop out the seeds, and cut into long slices.

PINEAPPLE
Choose fruit that gives a little near the leaves. Peel, remove the eyes and cut into wedges or slice into rounds.

POMELO
Grapefruit-like, it ranges from sweet to sour. Peel and separate it into segments and remove the papery skin. A pomelo should have filled-out skin, be fragrant, blemish-free, and heavy for its size. If unavailable, substitute pink or white grapefruit. Store in the refrigerator.

Entrance to Evans Pool. *Seattle Municipal Archives*

Chapter 4

Evans Pool
Swimmer's Dinner

My NEIGHBOR, FLORENCE, remembers trudging door to door with a tin can to raise money for the Evans Pool. The idea for a swimming pool in the north end of Seattle originated during the Depression. Funding was not forthcoming but years later the proposal resurfaced. In 1948 a determined group called the North End Pool Committee collected 50,000 signatures in support of a bond issue proposal. After five years and pressure from the PTA and other local organizations, the Park Board allocated funds for a pool with the stipulation that the cost could not exceed $250,000.

Completed in 1955, the pool was named in honor of the well-known Evans brothers. Ben Evans joined the Parks Department in 1917. He served as the director of recreation from 1938 to 1960 with his brother, Lou, as his assistant. Grand opening ceremonies featured comedy diving exhibitions by the Husky Swim Club and relay races by Roosevelt and Lincoln High Schools.

Today, for a modest fee, you can sign up for water exercise, take swimming lessons, or simply swim laps. Evans Pool offers a variety of lessons for all ages and abilities as well as recreational swims. The sauna can be used free of charge whenever the pool is open. Groups can rent the pool on a first-come-first-served basis. Call 206-684-4961 for reservations. The address is 7201 East Green Lake Drive North.

Adjacent to Evans Pool is the Green Lake Community Center, dedicated in 1929. Built over a garbage fill, the Community Center was funded by a $105,000 bond. Gifts from private firms, individuals, and associations including the PTA, furnished the building. It houses a gymnasium, showers, classrooms, and a weight room. Activities, many of which are free, include yoga, table tennis, volleyball, and basketball.

Have a swim party and continue the festivities in your kitchen with a hands-on pizza dinner. One of our most memorable get-togethers was a pizza party. Everyone brought a favorite topping and we supplied the rest. This menu lets everyone get into the act and create their own culinary master-piece—with or without anchovies. There is no wrong combination. Even the little ones can participate. The key to this dinner is advance prepara-tion. Have the sauce and accompaniments ready to go, and take the dough out of the refrigerator before you leave for the pool.

Planning a Pizza Party

The key to a successful party is organization. Begin by making a list of traditional and nontraditional toppings. Include a variety of meats, fish, vegetables, fruits, herbs, sauces and cheeses. For adventuresome eaters, buy items such as olive paste, Brie cheese, arugula, mint, capers, and prosciutto. Given the opportunity, people will create unusual combinations. At one of our parties, the big hit was Gorgonzola, pears, walnuts, and fresh mint. Ask guests in advance what kind of pizza they like, or ask them to bring a favorite topping.

A traditional pizza sauce should be included. *No-cook Tomato Sauce* is simple and quick; additional spices can be added to make a hotter sauce. Sauces and crusts can be purchased, but they seldom taste as good as home-made. The pizza dough should be prepared ahead of time and refrigerated after rising. Remove it about two hours before using. Have the pizza toppings ready before returning from the pool. Hungry guests can be immediately invited to roll out their pizzas, put on the toppings, and pop them in the oven.

Our favorite pizzas are listed below; the only limit is your imagination!

- Fresh basil, garlic, Brie, and tomatoes
- Smoked salmon, capers, goat cheese, and dill
- Portabello mushrooms, red peppers, and onions
- Gorgonzola, mint, pears, and walnuts
- Artichokes, feta, and tomatoes
- Goat cheese, marinated eggplant, and rosemary
- Pepper jack cheese, chorizo sausage, mushrooms, and onions
- Mozzarella, pesto, and shrimp

Party Pizza Dough

This dough can be made ahead of time and refrigerated.

1 package dry yeast
1 teaspoon sugar
1½ cups warm water
2 tablespoons olive oil
4 cups flour, or as needed
1½ teaspoons salt
1½ teaspoons fennel seeds (optional)

1. In a large bowl, dissolve the yeast and sugar into the warm water. Let stand 5 minutes, or until the yeast is foamy. Add the oil and mix well with a wooden spoon. Add 2 cups of the flour, salt, and fennel seeds; mix well. Add the remaining flour about ½ cup at a time, using your hands as needed. Add more flour if the dough is too sticky.

2. Turn the dough onto a lightly floured work surface. Knead 5 to 10 minutes, until the dough is smooth and elastic, adding just enough flour to keep it from sticking. Put the dough into a medium oiled bowl and place a damp cloth or lightly oiled plastic wrap over it. Let the dough rise in a warm area 1 to 1½ hours, until an impression remains when a finger is pressed into it.

3. Preheat the oven to 500 degrees. Turn the dough onto a lightly floured work surface and flatten it with the heel of your hand to remove air bubbles. Knead it a couple of times. Divide the dough into 6 equal portions and form into balls.* Cover and let rest about 15 minutes.

4. Sprinkle corn meal on a baking sheet or pizza paddle. With your hands or a rolling pin, form the dough into rounds about 8 inches in diameter, depending on the desired thickness. Add toppings as desired. Place the pizzas on a baking sheet or pizza stone and cook about 10 minutes, or until the crust is nicely browned. Serve immediately.

Yields 6 individual pizzas

---

*If not using the dough immediately, place the balls on a lightly oiled tray. Cover with lightly oiled plastic wrap and refrigerate. Remove about two hours before using, so dough comes to room temperature.

No-cook Tomato Sauce

Use this sauce as a base to make your own. Add red pepper flakes and other spices to suit your palate.

1 can (28 ounces) diced tomatoes in juice
2 cloves garlic, chopped
½ teaspoon dried basil
½ teaspoon dried oregano

Drain most of the liquid from the tomatoes and reserve. Process the ingredients in a food processor until smooth. If necessary, add some of the reserved tomato juice to thin the sauce. Add salt and freshly ground pepper to taste.

Yields about 2½ cups

Spicy Flatbread Sticks

An olive lover's favorite.

¾ cup finely grated Parmesan cheese
¼ teaspoon cayenne
½ teaspoon dried rosemary, crumbled
½ teaspoon salt
¾ cup warm water
1 package dry yeast
1½ cups flour, or as needed
½ cup kalamata olives, pitted and sliced in half

1. Combine the cheese, cayenne, rosemary, and salt in a small bowl; set aside.

2. Pour the warm water into a medium bowl. Add the yeast and stir with a wooden spoon until dissolved. Stir in one cup flour. Add the cheese mixture and as much of the remaining ½-cup flour as needed to form a soft dough. Add the olives and mix to distribute evenly.

3. Place dough on a floured work surface. Knead five minutes, or until the dough is elastic, adding enough flour so it isn't sticky. (It will turn light brown from the olives.) Cover with a damp cloth and let rise 20 minutes in a warm place. Preheat the oven to 375 degrees.

4. Using hands or a rolling pin, form the dough into a rectangle 8 x 14 inches. With a sharp knife, cut the dough crosswise into fourteen sticks. Stretching the dough as little as possible, put sticks on a baking sheet about 1 inch apart. Bake 20 minutes, or until the tops and bottoms are lightly browned. Serve immediately.

Yields 14 sticks

Spinach Salad with Warm Garlic Dressing

This salad can be made quickly if the prep work is done in advance.

SALAD
12 cups baby spinach leaves, washed and dried
8 medium mushrooms, washed, dried and thinly sliced
¼ cup pine nuts

DRESSING
⅓ cup extra virgin olive oil
1 large clove garlic, peeled
¼ teaspoon salt
3 tablespoons red wine vinegar
2 tablespoons chopped sun-dried tomatoes in olive oil, rinsed and patted
   dry

1. Combine the spinach, mushrooms, and pine nuts in a serving bowl.

2. To make dressing: in a small saucepan, heat the olive oil over medium-low heat. Meanwhile, mash the garlic with the salt using the tip of a knife. Add the garlic mixture to the olive oil and steep about five minutes. Remove from the heat.

3. Whisk in the vinegar. Add the sun-dried tomatoes and freshly ground pepper to taste; whisk well. Dress the salad; serve immediately.

Yields 6 servings

Biscotti with Mascarpone Cream and Strawberries

Mascarpone cream cheese is from the Lombardy region of Italy. Available in the dairy section of supermarkets and specialty stores.

6 plain or flavored biscotti, or 6 macaroon cookies
1¼ cups heavy whipping cream
1 teaspoon vanilla
2 tablespoons favorite liqueur, such as amaretto, or orange juice
⅓ cup superfine sugar
8 ounces mascarpone cream or ricotta cheese
1 pint medium strawberries, washed, hulled, and quartered, or other
   favorite fruit
Fresh mint for garnish

1. Crumble the biscotti into large crumbs (to give the dessert texture) and set aside.

2. Pour the whipping cream, vanilla, and liqueur into a medium bowl; whip on high until firm, gradually adding the sugar. Set aside.

3. Put the mascarpone cream into a large bowl and beat with a wooden spoon to soften. Fold in the whipping cream; chill until ready to serve.

4. Fold the biscotti and strawberries into the mascarpone cream mixture. Serve in parfait or other dessert glasses. Garnish with mint leaves.

Yields 6 to 8 servings

A little girl communes with the ducks on the north shore. *Susan Banks*

A 1999 Milk Carton Derby entry under youthful scrutiny. *Susan Banks*

Chapter 5

Seafair Milk Carton Derby Picnic

TAKE A PICNIC BASKET to the annual Milk Carton Derby, a Seafair event held the second Saturday in July. This unique event is one of many that has earned Seafair the distinction of being one of the top ten festivals in the United States. Other happenings include an air show featuring the Blue Angels, the Torchlight Parade, Hydroplane Races, Torchlight Run, and the Seafair Fleet Arrival and Tours.

Seafair was launched in the summer of 1950. Walter Van Camp, director of St. Paul's Winter Carnival in Minnesota, was hired to plan and publicize the festival. The first Milk Carton Derby race, billed as the International Milk Carton Boat Races, took its place in the lineup of events in 1972. At that time the Derby was not the only Seafair event held at Green Lake. The much-loved but noisy limited hydroplanes raced there until they were banned from Green Lake in 1984. (They now race at Lake Washington.)

At the Milk Carton Derby, you will see a hundred or so creative contraptions, made of empty milk cartons, battle to be first across the finish line. Despite a rule requiring entries to use at least 50 half-gallon plastic jugs or paper milk cartons, a few usually sink. (Participants are required to wear life preservers in case of a mishap.) Popular entries have included the Milky Way, the Moos Brothers, the Big Cheese, and the Titanic—complete with icebergs.

In addition to the races, there are lots of other activities for kids, including an ice-cream eating contest, milk carton sculpture center, and "moo off," in which young contestants moo into a microphone. Prizes are awarded to contest winners. Other events for youngsters are face painting, clowns, and arts and crafts.

The Seafair Milk Carton Derby runs from 10 a.m. until 4 p.m. and admission is free. The races are best viewed from the southwest shore of the lake. This festivity is popular, so plan to arrive early to find a good place for your picnic blanket.

As much as we love gourmet food, we're not snooty; we enjoy everything from hotdogs to hollandaise. At the Milk Carton Derby, vendor foods are available, but we created a menu with something special for the whole family. *Derby Turkey Empanadas* are just the right size for small hands. The healthy, grain *Captain's Couscous Salad* is a balanced meal in itself. If your children are fussy eaters, entice them to at least take a no-thank-you bite.

Avocado Mousse

Hass avocados are dark green with rough skin. Fuerte are lighter with a smooth, thin skin. Avocados turn brown when exposed to air, so be sure to make this the day of your picnic.

4 medium, ripe Hass avocados
½ cup whipping cream
2 tablespoons fresh lemon juice
1 fresh jalapeño chili pepper, or to taste, minced
2 cloves garlic, chopped
½ teaspoon salt
⅛ teaspoon chili powder

1. Cut the avocados in half and remove the seeds. Gently scoop out the flesh and break into chunks; reserve the skins. Set aside the avocado flesh.

2. Pour the whipping cream into a food processor or blender; process until it starts to become firm.

3. Add the avocado flesh, lemon juice, jalapeño, garlic, and salt to the whipping cream; process until smooth. Chill in the refrigerator at least one hour, or until very cold.

4. Mound the mousse into the reserved avocado skins and put in a covered container.* Cover tightly and pack in a cooler; keep chilled. Dust with chili powder. Serve with assorted chips.

Yields 6 to 8 servings

---

*The avocado mousse can also be served in a bowl, rather than in the avocado skins.

Nopales Corn Salsa

Nopales, or prickly pear cactus leaves, can be found in the Mexican section of most supermarkets. They lend an unusual flavor to this salsa.

2 cups corn kernels, preferably fresh
½ cup canned or bottled nopales, rinsed, drained, and diced (reserve juice)
2 plum tomatoes, seeded and diced

DRESSING
1 tablespoon cider vinegar
1 teaspoon juice from the nopales
2 cloves garlic, chopped
¼ cup vegetable oil

1. Combine the corn, nopales, and tomatoes in a medium bowl; set aside.

2. To make dressing: in a small bowl, whisk the cider vinegar, juice from the nopales, and garlic. Gradually whisk in the oil. Add salt and freshly ground pepper to taste.

3. Pour the dressing over the corn mixture; stir well. Adjust the seasoning if desired. Cover and chill in the refrigerator two hours. Put the salsa into a leakproof container and pack in a cooler. Serve with assorted chips, or serve as a side salad.

Yields 3 cups

Captain's Couscous Salad

After the slicing and dicing are done, this salad goes together quickly.

COUSCOUS
1¼ cups cold water
¼ teaspoon salt
1 cup quick-cooking couscous
1 can (15 ounces) black beans, rinsed and drained
1 red pepper, seeded and cut into ¼-inch dice
⅓ cup sliced green onions
1 can (2¼ ounces) sliced black olives, drained
¼ cup chopped fresh cilantro

DRESSING
⅓ cup fresh lemon juice
1 teaspoon chili powder
2 cloves garlic, finely chopped
½ teaspoon ground cumin
5 teaspoons sugar
½ teaspoon salt
⅓ cup vegetable oil

1. To make couscous: bring the water to a boil in a medium saucepan; add the salt. Gradually whisk in the couscous. Cover and remove from the heat. Let stand 5 to 10 minutes, until the water is absorbed, occasionally fluffing with a fork. Transfer to a large bowl.

2. To make dressing: combine the lemon juice, chili powder, garlic, cumin, sugar, and the ½ teaspoon salt in a small bowl. Whisk until the sugar and salt are dissolved. Gradually whisk in the vegetable oil; set aside.

3. Add the black beans, red pepper, green onions, olives, and cilantro to the couscous; mix well. Pour the dressing over the couscous and mix again; adjust the seasoning if desired. Cover and chill in the refrigerator 2 to 4 hours. Put in a leakproof container and pack in a cooler.

Yields 6 servings with other dishes in this menu

Derby Turkey Empanadas

This recipe can be doubled.

PASTRY
1½ cups flour
½ cup cornmeal
½ teaspoon ground cumin
1 teaspoon salt
4 tablespoons unsalted butter, chilled and diced
4 tablespoons vegetable shortening, chilled and diced
1 tablespoon lemon juice
5 to 6 tablespoons cold water, or as needed
1 egg, lightly beaten with 1 teaspoon cold water

FILLING
2 tablespoons vegetable oil
¼ cup finely chopped onion
2 cloves garlic, minced
½ pound ground turkey
¼ cup tomato sauce
⅓ cup dried currants or raisins
8 to 12 green olives stuffed with pimientos, sliced
½ teaspoon ground cinnamon
¼ teaspoon cayenne
¼ teaspoon salt

1. To make pastry: mix the flour, cornmeal, cumin, and salt in a large bowl. Cut the butter and shortening into the flour mixture with two knives or a pastry cutter, until it's the texture of small peas. Gradually add the lemon juice and enough water, tossing with a fork, until the dough just holds together; knead a few times. Divide into 6 balls. Cover and chill in the refrigerator 30 minutes.

2. To make filling: in a large skillet, heat the oil over medium heat. Add the onions and cook 5 minutes; add the garlic and cook briefly. Add the turkey and cook until lightly browned. Use a fork to break the turkey up into a fine texture.

3. Add the tomato sauce, currants, green olives, cinnamon, cayenne, and salt; stir well. Simmer 5 minutes; adjust the seasoning if desired. Remove from the heat. Preheat the oven to 375 degrees. Using your hands, flatten 1 ball of dough into a thick disk. Put it between two pieces of waxed paper. Roll dough into a round about ¼-inch thick. Peel the paper from the dough.

4. Spoon about 4 tablespoons of the filling into the center of the round. Dampen the edges with water. Stretch the dough over the filling and firmly seal the edges. Crimp with a fork. If the edge is ragged, trim with a knife. Brush the top evenly with the egg mixture; prick the top with a fork several times; place on a baking sheet. Repeat with the remaining dough. Bake 15 minutes, or until golden brown; cool 15 minutes. Chill in the refrigerator 2 hours. Put in a covered container and pack in a cooler; keep chilled. When we serve these at home, we prefer them warm or at room temperature.

Yields 6 empanadas

Fresh Fruit Kebabs with Creamy Dip

Avoid fruit that turns brown or mushy, such as bananas, pears, or apples.

FRUITS
Select firm fruits such as seedless grapes, nectarines, pineapple, melon, and strawberries

DIP
4 ounces Neufchâtel or cream cheese
½ teaspoon vanilla
½ teaspoon coconut extract
8 ounces fat-free plain yogurt
½ cup sweetened, shredded or flaked coconut

1. Peel and cube the fruit as necessary. Thread on wooden skewers and pack in a cooler.

2. Put the Neufchâtel in a food processor and process briefly. Add the vanilla, coconut extract, and yogurt. Pulse until just blended; remove and add the coconut; mix well. Chill in the refrigerator 2 hours. Spoon dip into a covered container and pack in a cooler; keep chilled. Serve with fruit kebabs.

Yields 1½ cups dip

Seafair Milk Carton Derby entries, 1970s. *Courtesy of Seafair*

Powder Puff Hydroplane Race at Green Lake, July 30, 1965. *Seattle PI Collection, Museum of History and Industry*

Chapter 6

Children's Paddleboat Party

D URING THE SUMMER, weather permitting, you can rent paddleboats, canoes, kayaks, sailboards, rowboats, or sailboats at the northeast end of the lake. The paddleboats are especially fun for the children. Let them pump the pedals while the adults relax.

The first paddleboats on the lake, called Water Kings, were built by Mr. H.O. Wilson in Carson City, Nevada. The invention looked like a cross between a tandem bike and a pontoon boat. Foot pedals operated a propeller and handlebars controlled the rudder. Top speed was about 5 knots. A concession of Water Kings operated at Green Lake briefly in the early 1940s.

Boating on Green Lake has had a long and controversial history. Some races, including the Model Boat Competition, Speedboat Regatta, Water Ski Tournament, and Seafair Hydroplane Race, aggravated the neighborhood. Green Lake residents complained about the noise, many writing letters of protest to the Park Board. For safety reasons, it eventually became necessary to limit the number of boats on the lake. In 1953 the Board passed a policy prohibiting the use of privately owned boats on Green Lake from June 1st through Labor Day, except for special events. In 1984 the Seafair hydroplanes were banned because of the noise and for environmental reasons. Today, quieter watercraft dot the lake on a sunny day. Boating lessons for all ages are available at the Small Craft Center on the south shore.

The lake is kept open for boating and swimming primarily by a peculiar-looking machine called an aquatic plant harvester. It performs a function vital to the health of the lake by cutting weeds, mainly Eurasion milfoil. The weeds are loaded onto a deck, taken to shore, and recycled into compost.

After turning in the paddleboats and life preservers, round up the crew and have lunch at one of the nearby picnic tables. Afterwards, children can burn up excess energy at the play area near the Community Center, built with funds from the Forward Thrust bond measure. In 1996, the equipment was replaced at a cost of about $182,000. Fun playthings include a canoe, baby bucket seats, sand toys, talk tube, and swings, designed with maximum safety in mind. The site also meets requirements for the Americans with Disabilities Act.

We went straight to the source for this menu: kids! Our informal survey indicated that they prefer uncomplicated, comfort-type foods: pasta salads, homemade sandwiches, and cookies. We designed this menu to satisfy everyone. Adults will enjoy the *Little Devil Sandwiches,* too—but don't tell the kids!

Garden Herb Dip

This is a healthy dip even most children will like. Other herbs, such as tarragon, oregano, and mint, can be substituted.

8 ounces light or fat-free sour cream
¼ cup light Miracle Whip or mayonnaise
½ cucumber, peeled, seeded, and chopped
2 tablespoons fresh lemon juice
½ cup coarsely chopped green onions
1 tablespoon chopped fresh parsley
1 tablespoon chopped fresh dill weed, or 1 teaspoon dried
1 tablespoon chopped fresh basil, or 1 teaspoon dried

1. Process the sour cream, Miracle Whip, cucumber, and lemon juice in a food processor or blender, until the mixture is just a little chunky. Add the green onions, parsley, dill, and basil. Pulse a few times to incorporate. Add salt and pepper to taste.

2. Pour into a covered container and chill 2 hours in the refrigerator. Pack in a cooler and keep chilled. Serve with baby carrots, cucumber, zucchini spears, or other fresh vegetables suitable for dipping.

Yields 1½ cups

Little Devil Sandwiches

Make one or both fillings. The recipes can be doubled.

1 loaf French bread, or similar bread, about 16" long x 5½" wide

DEVILED HAM FILLING
½ pound cooked ham, coarsely chopped
4 ounces cream cheese, cut into pieces
2 tablespoons coarsely chopped green onions
1 tablespoon honey mustard
1 teaspoon Worcestershire sauce
3 dashes Tabasco, or to taste

SMOKED TURKEY FILLING
½ pound smoked turkey, coarsely chopped
6 ounces cream cheese, cut into pieces
3 tablespoons chopped shallots
½ teaspoon dried thyme
⅛ teaspoon pepper
¼ cup whole berry cranberry sauce

1. Cut the bread in half **crosswise.** Hollow out both halves, leaving a 1-inch border of bread on all sides.

2. To make ham filling: put the ham, cream cheese, green onions, mustard, Worcestershire sauce, and Tabasco into a food processor. Process until smooth. Add pepper to taste.

3. To make turkey filling: put the turkey, cream cheese, shallots, thyme, and pepper into a food processor. Process until smooth; spoon into a bowl and add the cranberry sauce. Stir until just mixed. Add salt to taste.

4. Spoon the filling into the hollowed bread halves. Press down gently to ensure the filling is completely to the end and covering the hollowed area. Place the filled ends of the halves together and press firmly. Wrap securely with plastic wrap. Chill in the refrigerator 2 to 4 hours, until the filling is firm. Pack in a cooler and keep chilled. Slice and serve with sweet or hot mustards and cranberry sauce.

Yields 12 sandwiches

Racer's Rotini Salad

This pasta salad is loaded with some of children's favorite foods—bacon, cheese, and apples.

1 tablespoon salt
½ pound dried rotini pasta
½ pound medium cheddar cheese, cubed
1 large red apple, such as Red Delicious, cored and cubed
6 strips thick bacon, fried, drained, and cut into ½-inch pieces
½ cup ranch dressing

1. In a large pot, bring about 4 quarts water to a rapid boil and add the salt. Add the pasta and boil until slightly firm, about seven minutes. Drain and put in a large bowl; cool briefly.

2. Add the cheese, apple, and bacon; stir. Pour the ranch dressing on top; mix well. Add salt and pepper to taste. Chill in the refrigerator 2 to 4 hours. Put in a covered container and pack in a cooler; keep chilled.

Yields 6 six servings with other dishes in this menu

Five-Spice Fruit Medley

Five-spice powder is used in Chinese cooking. It's a combination of cinnamon, cloves, fennel seed, star anise, and Sichuan peppercorns.

1 carton (8 ounces) plain yogurt
3 tablespoons strawberry jam, warmed until liquid
1 teaspoon honey, or to taste
Generous pinch Chinese five-spice, or a pinch each of cinnamon, cloves, and pepper
½ cantaloupe, cubed
1 pint medium strawberries, washed, stemmed, and halved
2 bananas, sliced
1 cup purple grapes

1. Strain yogurt: place a colander in a bowl or pan and line the colander with several layers of cheesecloth. Spoon the yogurt into the cheesecloth-lined colander and strain for thirty minutes in the refrigerator; discard the liquid.

2. Combine the strained yogurt, strawberry jam, honey, and five-spice powder in a small bowl. Place the fruit in a large bowl and pour the dressing on top; mix gently. Chill in the refrigerator 2 hours. Put in a leakproof container and pack in a cooler. Keep chilled.

Yields 6 servings

Crazy Pizza Cookie

This giant brownie cookie can be topped with anything that appeals to kids—coconut, M&Ms, flavored chips, sprinkles, or nuts.

2 ounces semi-sweet baking chocolate
1 stick (½ cup) butter
1 tablespoon unsweetened cocoa
1 cup sugar
1 cup flour, sifted
¼ teaspoon salt
2 eggs, lightly beaten
1 teaspoon vanilla
½ cup walnuts, chopped (optional)
½ cup sweetened, shredded or flaked coconut
⅓ cup raspberry or other flavored chips
⅓ cup mini M&Ms (baking bits)
12-inch pizza pan

1. Preheat the oven to 350 degrees. Line a 12-inch pizza pan with foil and butter generously. Melt the baking chocolate and the ½-cup butter in a microwave on medium heat for 1 minute, or until melted. Add the cocoa; mix thoroughly. Set aside.

2. Combine the sugar, flour, and salt in a medium bowl. Add the chocolate and butter mixture, eggs, and vanilla; mix well. Add the walnuts, coconut, half of the flavored chips and half of the M&Ms. Mix until evenly dispersed.

3. Pour the batter onto the lined pizza pan and spread evenly. Sprinkle the remaining flavored chips and M&Ms over the batter and press in lightly with the back of a spoon. Bake 25 to 30 minutes, or until a toothpick inserted into the center comes out clean.

4. Cool thoroughly on the pan, about an hour. Invert on a large plate and carefully peel off the aluminum foil. Invert back on to the pizza pan. Cut into 12 wedges. Pack in an airtight container.

Yields 12 cookie wedges

Berry Good Lemonade

For the best results, add the 7up right before you serve it.

1 can (12 ounces) frozen pink lemonade concentrate
4 cups plus ¼ cup cold water
1 cup frozen mixed berries
3 to 4 cups 7up

1. In a pitcher, combine the lemonade with the 4 cups water; mix well.

2. Bring the remaining ¼ cup water to a boil in a small saucepan. Add the berries and simmer 5 minutes, or until very soft. Strain the mixture and reserve the liquid; cool about 10 minutes.

3. Add the berry liquid to the lemonade; mix well. Chill in the refrigerator; pour into an insulated thermos. Add the 7up immediately before serving and stir.

Yields about 2 quarts

Children's Swimming Bath and Boat House in the early 1900s at Woodland Park, south Green Lake. *MSCUA, Univ. of Washington Libraries, Neg. UW 4727*

Stewart Terry fills luminarias with sand along the pathway, 1999. *Susan Banks*

Chapter 7

Pathway of Lights Luminarias Dinner

A COMMUNITY ISN'T DEFINED by physical boundaries but rather by the events and celebrations that draw neighbors together. The spirit of Green Lake shines its brightest in December, when dancing luminarias encircle the lake like a warm embrace. The annual Pathway of Lights is a relatively new event, first sponsored in 1984 by the Green Lake Community Center and the Advisory Council. This tradition, borrowed from the American Southwest, has grown to become a holiday attraction for the whole city. Thousands join in the celebration held the second Saturday in December.

Excellent organization and a multitude of volunteers are needed to light up the pathway. On the afternoon of the event, people gather in the Community Center gymnasium and are assigned to a team. Each team is responsible for one of eleven zones where sand has already been dumped. Supplied with a wheelbarrow, shovels, bags, and tea lights, team members fill and place the bags about six feet apart on both sides of the pathway, in assembly-line fashion. In all, about 6,000 bags line the circumference of the lake and fishing piers. At 6 p.m., volunteers return to light the candles— a daunting task when the Pacific Northwest weather doesn't cooperate.

If the forecast is for showers, arrive at the lake when the luminarias are lighted and plan to have dinner afterwards. Stop by the Community Center to hear Christmas music. This tradition dates to the seventies when children from local elementary schools sang on the nearby beach. Stroll the pathway and join neighbors singing their favorite songs. Look for dogs twinkling red and green, grownups wearing antlers, and Santa Claus. Boats trimmed with lights, a miniature version of the Parade of Lights on Lake Washington, glide near the shores.

The shimmering luminarias are spectacular, especially when the weather is clear. Typically, though, it rains. December in Seattle is usually wet and breezy. The show goes on despite the weather.

During the holidays, our thoughts turn toward formal foods that require a minimum amount of preparation. Welcome dinner guests with luminarias on your porch and bring the glow indoors with plenty of glimmering candles. The first course for this dinner, creamy *Champagne Mustard Soup,* will quickly warm up the group. *Lamb Kebabs,* rich in flavor without being heavy, are complemented by *Rosemary Walnut Rice* and *Tangy Carrot Coins.* Colorful *Raspberry Almond Crisp* tops off the festive meal.

Champagne Mustard Soup

If you can't find champagne mustard, substitute Dijon honey mustard.

2 tablespoons unsalted butter
1 shallot, finely chopped
2 tablespoons flour
2 teaspoons dry mustard
Pinch of turmeric
5 cups homemade chicken broth or fat-free canned
1 large russet potato (about 1 pound), peeled and cut into ½-inch cubes
1 tablespoon fresh lemon juice
2 tablespoons plus 2 teaspoons champagne mustard or Dijon honey mustard
Pinch of white pepper (optional)
¼ cup whipping cream, warmed
2 tablespoons chopped chives for garnish

1. Melt the butter in a medium heavy-bottomed saucepan over medium-low heat. Slowly sauté the shallots until softened, about 5 minutes. Increase the heat to medium and gradually whisk in the flour. Cook about 2 minutes, whisking constantly. Whisk in the dry mustard and turmeric.

2. Gradually whisk in the chicken stock; add the potatoes and bring to a boil. Reduce the heat and simmer uncovered until tender, about 15 minutes. Cool briefly.

3. In two batches, puree the soup solids with about 2 cups of the liquid (per batch). Whisk the pureed mixture back into the remaining liquids in the pan over medium heat. Add the lemon juice, champagne mustard, and white pepper; whisk well. Stir in the cream and remove from the heat; add salt to taste. Serve in warmed bowls. Garnish with chopped chives.

Yields 6 servings

Christmas Crackers

Green onions and pimientos make this cracker festive. You can prepare them a day ahead and store them in an airtight container.

2 cups flour
½ teaspoon salt
2 tablespoons unsalted butter, chilled
⅓ cup cold water, or as needed
2 tablespoons fresh lemon juice
¼ cup thinly sliced green onions (green part only)
¼ cup pimientos, drained, coarsely chopped, and thoroughly dried
Coarse salt

1. Preheat the oven to 350 degrees. Combine the flour and salt in a medium bowl. Cut the butter into small pieces, add to the flour mixture, and coat. Using a pastry blender or two knives, cut the butter into the flour until the pieces are the size of coarse cornmeal.

2. Pour most of the water and the lemon juice over the flour mixture; toss it with a fork until large clumps form. Add more of the water as needed to form a soft (but not sticky) dough. Add the green onions, working them into the dough. Form the dough into a disk.

3. Lightly flour a work surface. Cut the dough into two equal pieces. Roll one piece into a rectangle as thin as possible, about ¹/₁₆-inch thick. Sprinkle half of the pimientos evenly over the top of the dough and carefully press them into it with a rolling pin. Cut off the ragged edges with a knife.

4. Carefully lift the dough onto a baking sheet. Using a pizza cutter or a sharp knife, score the dough into 2-inch squares. Prick each square with a fork a couple of times. Sprinkle lightly with coarse salt. Bake 15 minutes, or until lightly browned and crisp. Repeat with the remaining dough. Cool on a rack; break into squares. Serve immediately, or put in a container and cover tightly.

Yields about 75 crackers

Minty Grilled Lamb Kebabs

If serving hearty eaters, increase the amount of lamb to 3 pounds.

MARINADE
½ cup lightly packed fresh mint
½ cup lightly packed Italian parsley
⅔ cup extra virgin olive oil
5 cloves garlic, peeled
1 tablespoon fresh lemon juice
1 tablespoon low-sodium soy sauce
¾ teaspoon coarse salt
½ teaspoon freshly ground pepper

2½ pounds lamb sirloin or boneless leg of lamb (preferably sirloin), cut
    into 1½-inch pieces
Metal skewers

1. To make marinade: put all the ingredients except for the lamb into a
   food processor. Process until the texture is a little coarse. Put the lamb
   into a medium glass bowl, and pour the marinade on top. Mix well and
   cover. Marinate in the refrigerator 2 to 4 hours, stirring occasionally.

2. Preheat the broiler. Thread about 5 pieces of lamb onto each skewer.
   Discard the marinade. Broil about 5 minutes on each side for medium,
   or until done. Serve over Rosemary Walnut Rice.

Yields 6 servings

Rosemary Walnut Rice

This elegant rice is easy to make. The nut mixture can be prepared ahead of time and reheated in a microwave oven before adding it to the rice.

NUT MIXTURE
1 tablespoon unsalted butter
½ cup walnuts, chopped
1 teaspoon dried rosemary
¼ teaspoon salt

RICE
3 cups cold water
½ teaspoon salt
3 cups long-grain white instant rice
3 tablespoons chopped parsley

1. To make nuts: melt the butter over medium-low heat in a small sauté pan. Add the walnuts, rosemary and the ¼ teaspoon salt. Cook until the nuts are nicely browned, about ten minutes; set aside.

2. To make rice: bring the water to a boil; add the ½ teaspoon salt. Stir in the rice and cover. Remove from the heat and let stand 5 minutes, or until the water is absorbed. Stir in the parsley and the nut mixture. Serve immediately.

Yields 6 servings

Tangy Carrot Coins

When balsamic vinegar is reduced, it thickens and becomes sweet. An expensive brand is not required for this recipe.

1 pound carrots, peeled and cut into ¼ inch slices
1 cup canned fat-free chicken stock
¼ cup balsamic vinegar
½ teaspoon fresh lemon juice
⅛ teaspoon dried basil, crumbled
1 teaspoon sugar

Steam the carrots in a steamer over the chicken stock until crisp-tender; remove from the heat. Meanwhile, bring the vinegar to a boil and reduce it to two tablespoons. Whisk in the lemon juice, basil, and sugar. Add salt and pepper to taste. Toss the carrots in the sauce. Serve immediately, or refrigerate and reheat.

Yields 6 servings

Raspberry Almond Crisp

Serve warm with a dollop of good-quality vanilla ice cream.

FILLING
3 12-ounce packages frozen raspberries, thawed, or 6 cups fresh
½ cup sugar
1 teaspoon almond extract
½ cup flour

TOPPING
1 cup packed brown sugar
1 cup flour
¾ cup regular or quick rolled oats
1 teaspoon ground cinnamon
1 stick (½ cup) unsalted butter, room temperature, cut into pieces
½ cup sliced almonds

1. For filling: preheat the oven to 375 degrees. Butter an 8 x 8-inch baking
   pan. If using frozen raspberries, drain them. In a medium bowl, gently
   mix the raspberries, sugar, and almond extract. Sprinkle the flour over
   the mixture and gently mix well. Spoon the mixture into the pan.

2. For topping: combine the brown sugar, flour, rolled oats, and cinnamon
   in a medium bowl. Using a pastry blender, work the butter into the
   mixture. (It will be crumbly.) Add the almonds and mix well. Sprinkle
   the topping evenly over the filling. Bake 30 minutes, or until fruit is
   bubbling and the top is golden. Serve with whipped cream or vanilla ice
   cream.

Yields 6 to 9 servings

Winter scene in 1903, with the McDonald home across the lake in the background. *MSCUA, Univ. of Washington Libraries, Neg. UW 1630*

1960s Green Lake crew team carrying an eight-oar shell. *Seattle Parks and Recreation. Photo by Charlie Heib.*

Chapter 8

Breakfast Before
the Regatta

I N ANCHORAGE, where we both lived for many years, spring is called breakup, trees don't bud until May, and some years it snows on Easter. After moving to Seattle, we quickly discovered the rumors were true. It rains a lot! We're just grateful we don't have to shovel the stuff. In spite of the drizzle, activities at Green Lake, including boating, go on as if it were warm enough to get a suntan.

The three annual regattas hosted by the Rowing Advisory Council will inspire landlubbers and water buffs alike. The first race of the season is the Spring Rowing Regatta, held in March. Races include Juniors, Masters, and Open athletes and begin at the north end of Green Lake. The length of the course is 1000 meters. A good spot to view them is from the Aqua Center at the south end of the lake, where the races end. If you miss the Spring Regatta, attend the Summer Rowing Extravaganza held in August; chocolate chip cookies are among the coveted awards. The Frostbite Regatta held in November draws competitors from throughout the Northwest.

The youth rowing program was established in 1947. Adult programs were added in 1984 and have been popular ever since. There are classes for youth and adults at every level, from the weekend boater to the experienced. If you have the energy and the ambition, you can learn to sail, canoe, kayak, and row without leaving the city!

The original site of the Green Lake Crew program was the Conroy Boathouse on the eastern shore. In 1950 the crew program moved into a new facility near the Aqua Theatre, the Massart Shellhouse. Named after Clarence Massart, a city council member and founder of the Wallingford Boys Club, it was built at the same time as the Aqua Theatre at no cost to the city. Fifteen years later, the Shellhouse was severely damaged in the 1965 earthquake. When the building was repaired, additional shell storage was added to accommodate the growth of the crew program. The most recent expansion was completed in 1980 with funds from a Forward Thrust Bond. The Green Lake Small Craft Center was built, the Massart Shellhouse underwent another remodel, and the Aqua Theatre was partially demolished.

In the late 1960s, two public clubs, the Seattle Canoe Club and the Seattle Sailing Association, decided to make Green Lake their home. Canoeing and sailing were added to the rowing classes already offered by the Small Craft Center. Volunteers from both clubs have formed successful partnerships with the Seattle Department of Parks and Recreation. Their presence was a major factor in the expansion of the Small Craft Center. For information about the regattas or classes, call the Center at 206-684-4074. Their address is 5900 West Green Lake Way North.

In recent years, Seattle has earned a reputation for fine dining and continues to attract innovative chefs. Seafood so fresh it fairly quivers is featured on menus throughout the city. Our *Northwest Oven Omelet,* showcasing smoked salmon, is sure to be a favorite with Seattleites and out-of-town guests.

Pike Place, the quintessential farmer's market, attracts tourists and food aficionados alike. Spend the day wandering about, filling your basket with items for this Northwest brunch. Organically grown vegetables, with dirt still clinging to the roots, are readily available. Select food from the low stalls where produce is likely to have been picked that morning. Lush bouquets of flowers are also available.

Northwest Oven Omelets

For an elegant presentation, bake these in individual soufflé dishes.

10 eggs
½ cup milk
4 ounces smoked salmon, flaked
1 cup (4 ounces) grated medium cheddar Tillamook cheese
4 ounces light cream cheese, cut into small pieces
3 tablespoons small capers, rinsed and drained
¼ teaspoon white pepper
¼ teaspoon salt
Dill sprigs for garnish

1. Preheat the oven to 375 degrees. Oil 6 individual soufflé dishes (10 ounces each), or an 8 x 8-inch baking dish. In a large bowl, whisk the eggs and milk. Add the salmon, cheddar cheese, cream cheese, capers, white pepper, and salt; mix well.

2. Divide the egg mixture between the soufflé dishes. Lay sprigs of dill on top in a decorative fashion. Bake 30 minutes, or until the center of each omelet is firm and the sides have pulled away. Serve immediately.

Yields 6 servings

Good Morning Scones with Honey Orange Butter

Toasting the nuts is not necessary, but it makes them more flavorful.

SCONES
2⅔ cups flour
½ cup sugar
2 teaspoons baking powder
1 teaspoon baking soda
½ teaspoon salt
6 tablespoons unsalted butter, chilled and cut into small pieces
½ cup milk
2 eggs
½ cup dried cranberries
½ cup walnuts, [toasted] and chopped
Finely grated zest of 1 orange

HONEY ORANGE BUTTER
1 stick (½ cup) unsalted butter, softened
2 teaspoons orange juice
½ teaspoon vanilla extract
4 teaspoons honey

1. Preheat the oven to 400 degrees. Combine the flour, sugar, baking powder, baking soda, and salt in a large bowl. Add the butter and coat it with the flour mixture. Using a pastry cutter or two knives, cut it into the flour mixture until it resembles small peas.

2. Whisk the milk and eggs in a medium bowl. Add to the dry ingredients and mix with a wooden spoon until just moistened. Add the cranberries, walnuts, and orange zest; mix until dispersed. Knead a few times.

3. Put the dough on an ungreased baking sheet. Form into an 8-inch round. Using a sharp knife, deeply score into fourths and then eighths. Dust with flour. Bake 20 minutes, or until browned and a toothpick inserted into the center comes out clean. Cool briefly before cutting.

4. To make butter: In a small bowl, beat the butter with a wooden spoon until fluffy. Add the orange juice, vanilla, and honey; mix well. Cover and chill in a small bowl, or put the butter on plastic wrap and form into a cylinder. Chill and cut into slices when ready to use.

Yields 8 scones and about ½ cup butter

Artichoke and Onion Potatoes

The potatoes can be steamed ahead of time.

1½ pounds small red potatoes
2 tablespoons unsalted butter
1 tablespoon olive oil
1 cup frozen pearl onions, thawed, or canned baby onions
1 jar (6½ ounces) marinated artichoke hearts, rinsed, drained and quartered
2 cloves garlic, minced
3 tablespoons chopped parsley

Steam the potatoes until just tender, about 15 minutes; cool and quarter. Heat the butter and oil in a large frying pan over medium-high heat. Add the potatoes, onions, artichokes hearts, and garlic. Cook quickly, until the potatoes are nicely browned. Add salt and freshly ground pepper to taste. Remove from the stove and stir in the parsley; serve immediately.

Yields 6 servings

Crewman's Fruit Cup

Natural and not overly sweet.

3½ pounds cooking apples, such as Rome Beauty, peeled, cored, and
 coarsely chopped
½ cup packed brown sugar
½ teaspoon cinnamon
1 cup water
2 pints strawberries, washed, dried, and hulled

1. Put the apples in a large saucepan. Add the brown sugar, cinnamon,
   and water; mix well. Bring to a boil. Reduce the heat and simmer
   uncovered until the apples are tender but not mushy, about 20 minutes.
   Stir occasionally. Remove from the heat. Using a potato masher or a
   pastry blender, mash the apples to a chunky consistency.

2. Meanwhile, put the strawberries into a food processor. Process until not
   quite smooth. Add the strawberries to the apples and mix well. Add
   additional sugar if desired. Serve warm or cold.

Yields about 6 cups

Women on an autumn nature walk at Green Lake, ca. 1908. *MSCUA, Univ. of Washington Libraries, Neg. UW 4724*

Chapter 9

Nature Walk Picnic

S OMETIMES WHEN WALKING around the lake on a sunny day, I forget that just beyond the bustling pathway is a thriving ecosystem. Birds mate and build nests, trees die and attract insects, and birds eat the insects. Although the natural habitat has been disturbed by the human population, numerous species of trees and waterfowl thrive. When you take the time to explore, the park becomes an urban laboratory.

A self-guided tree walk is available at the lake, thanks to the Green Lake Park Alliance, which completed a project in 1997 to label 133 species of trees. For a small donation at the Community Center, you can acquire a copy of the award-winning brochure *The Trees of Green Lake, A Walking Tour*. Inside is a detailed map of the lake with numbers corresponding to trees along the pathway. The trees are identified with small tags.

Of the approximately 162 species of trees at Green Lake, only fifteen are native, notes Arthur Lee Jacobson in his book, *Trees of Green Lake*. Of particular interest are the Black Walnut trees along West Green Lake Way, planted to commemorate local soldiers killed in World War I. In the spring, flowering cherry trees donated by the Japanese Association of America in 1930 grace the perimeter. Near the Bathhouse Theatre, the Habitat Enhancement Project has preserved land with snags (dead standing trees) to provide a more suitable habitat for birds, insects, and animals.

The tree population continues to evolve. Every year, the Seattle Department of Parks and Recreation removes trees that are old, damaged, or deemed unsuitable for the park. New ones chosen for their beauty and durability are planted in conjunction with the Green Lake Park Alliance Reforestation Committee.

October through April, local biologist Martin Muller leads free bird watching tours the first and third Saturdays of the month. Muller's enthusiasm is contagious, even for those not keen on birds, and his knowledge of the area is extensive. Between bird sightings, Muller often shares a local history lesson and discusses the ecology of Green Lake.

With a little practice one can learn to identify gulls, widgeons, American coots, Canada geese, red-winged blackbirds, and more. Sometimes hawks or eagles are observed. According to Muller, about 160 species of birds have been sighted; in the winter the variety averages at about forty. Summer months yield fewer species sightings, due to nesting habits. Those interested in a tour should call the Green Lake Park Alliance at 206-985-9235 for dates and times. Group size is limited to fifteen.

The tours go on regardless of inclement weather so dress appropriately. No experience is required, but binoculars are highly recommended. Groups meet at the lifeguard station on the east beach at 8 a.m. A note of caution: human food is harmful to the waterfowl; don't give in to the temptation to feed them.

With the availability of natural, healthy foods, it's easy to eat vegetarian without feeling deprived. It's not about restraint, but rather refocusing on what constitutes a meal. One of our favorite salads, *Tabouleh Salad with Feta,* is the centerpiece of this menu. The nutty flavor of bulgur wheat is enhanced with plenty of herbs. Feta cheese and kalamata olives give it a pleasing tang. After you've finished the main course, bite into a *Nature Date Bar* and sip a cup of *Meditation Tea* while you listen to the cheery chatter of birds.

Red Pepper Soup

Buy the peppers already roasted if you're short on time.

3 medium red peppers, or 7 ounces roasted red peppers
2 cans (14½ ounces each) vegetable broth
1¼ cups water
1 white potato (8 ounces), peeled and cubed
½ cup chopped onion
2 carrots (about 6 ounces total), peeled and sliced into ¼-inch pieces
¼ cup tomato paste
⅛ teaspoon cayenne, or to taste
Grated Parmesan cheese for garnish

1. Preheat the broiler if you are roasting the peppers. Cut tops and bottoms off the peppers, slice in half, seed and remove the ribs. Place them on a lightly oiled baking sheet skin side up. Broil about 10 minutes, or until blackened. If necessary, turn the pan to ensure the peppers blacken evenly. Remove from the oven and put in a paper bag. Close tightly and let stand 20 minutes. Remove from the bag; peel off the blackened skin and discard.

2. Cut the roasted peppers into 1½-inch squares. Put red peppers, vegetable broth, water, potatoes, onion, carrots, tomato paste, and cayenne in a medium saucepan; bring to a boil. Reduce the heat and simmer 30 minutes, or until the vegetables are soft, stirring occasionally. Remove from heat and cool. Process soup in a blender or food processor (in three batches) until smooth. Serve hot or cold. Pour into an insulated thermos. Garnish with Parmesan cheese.

Yields 6 cups

Tabouleh Salad with Feta

This salad can also be made with rice or quinoa. Follow the cooking directions on the package.

1 cup bulgur wheat
2 cups boiling water
1 small cucumber, peeled, seeded, and diced
2 roma or plum tomatoes (about ½ pound), seeded and chopped
¼ cup chopped green onions
¼ cup chopped fresh mint
⅔ cup kalamata olives, pitted
4 ounces feta cheese, diced
¼ cup chopped parsley

DRESSING
¼ cup fresh lemon juice (1 to 2 lemons)
¼ cup olive oil
2 cloves garlic, chopped
½ teaspoon salt
¼ teaspoon freshly ground pepper

1. Put the bulgur wheat into a large, heatproof bowl and pour the boiling water over it; cover with a heatproof plate. Let stand one hour; drain liquid if necessary.

2. To make dressing: in a small bowl, whisk the lemon juice, olive oil, garlic, salt, and pepper; set aside.

3. Add the cucumber, tomatoes, green onions, mint, olives, feta, and parsley to the bulgur wheat; mix well. Pour the dressing over it and mix again. Chill in the refrigerator 2 hours. Put the tabouleh in a leakproof container and pack in a cooler; keep chilled.

Yields 6 servings

Northern White Bean Spread with Caramelized Onions

Caramelized onions add richness to this spread.

1 can (15 ounces) Great Northern white beans
1 tablespoon olive oil
1 small onion, thinly sliced
½ cup light or regular sour cream
4 teaspoons fresh lemon juice
1 teaspoon dried marjoram
¼ teaspoon dried thyme
¼ teaspoon freshly ground pepper

1. Rinse the beans and drain them. Heat the olive oil in a medium sauté pan over medium heat. Add the onions and reduce the heat to medium-low. Slowly cook them 30 minutes, or until they are deeply browned, but not burned; set aside.

2. Combine the beans, sour cream, lemon juice, marjoram, thyme, and pepper in a food processor or blender; process briefly. Add the onions and blend well; add salt to taste. Cover and chill in the refrigerator 2 hours. Pack in a cooler and keep chilled.

Yields 1½ cups

Roasted Garlic Pita Chips

Another flavored oil, such at hot chili, can be substituted.

1 large whole head of garlic
⅓ cup plus 1 teaspoon extra virgin olive oil
5 white or whole-wheat pita bread pockets

1. Preheat the oven to 350 degrees. Remove most of the papery white skin from the garlic. (The cloves should not fall apart). Cut off the top of the head to expose the cloves. Place on a double layer of aluminum foil. Drizzle with the 1 teaspoon olive oil; season with salt and freshly ground pepper. Wrap loosely with the foil.

2. Bake in a small, heatproof dish 50 minutes, or until very soft. Remove garlic from the foil; cool until you can handle it. Squeeze the cloves into a small bowl. Add the olive oil and whisk thoroughly, breaking up the garlic. Let stand 30 minutes.

3. Cut each pita pocket into fourths; cut or tear each fourth in half. Brush the rough side of each pita triangle with the oil, letting bits of garlic cling to them. Place on a baking sheet, rough side up; bake 10 minutes, or until crisp and lightly browned. Cool and store in an airtight container.

Yields 40 chips

Nature Date Bars

Satisfying but not overly rich.

1 cup flour
½ cup regular or quick rolled oats
⅓ cup packed brown sugar
1 cup chopped dried dates (about 16 whole pitted dates)
⅓ cup chopped dried pears or dried apricots
½ cup unsweetened or sweetened flaked coconut
½ cup walnuts, chopped
¼ teaspoon baking soda
¼ teaspoon baking powder
1 teaspoon ground cinnamon
¼ teaspoon salt
2 eggs, lightly beaten
¼ cup canola oil
3 tablespoons apple juice

1. Preheat the oven to 350 degrees. Lightly oil an 8 x 8-inch baking pan. Combine the flour, oats, brown sugar, dates, pears, coconut, walnuts, baking soda, baking powder, cinnamon, and salt in a medium bowl.

2. Combine the eggs, canola oil, and apple juice in a separate bowl. Add to the dry ingredients and mix until just blended. Spread the mixture evenly in the pan. Bake 25 minutes, or until the top is lightly browned and the edges pull away from the pan. Cool and cut into 16 bars. Pack in an airtight container.

Yields 16 bars

Naughty Nature Date Bars

A richer version of our bars.

1 cup flour
½ cup regular or quick rolled oats
½ cup packed brown sugar plus 2 tablespoons for the topping
1 cup chopped dried dates (about 16 whole pitted dates)
½ cup sweetened flaked coconut
¼ teaspoon baking soda
¼ teaspoon baking powder
1 teaspoon ground cinnamon
2 tablespoons chopped candied ginger plus two tablespoons for the topping
½ cup walnuts, chopped
1 egg, lightly beaten
6 tablespoons unsalted butter, softened

1. Preheat the oven to 350 degrees. Oil an 8 x 8-inch baking pan. Combine the flour, oats, ½ cup of the brown sugar, dates, coconut, baking soda, baking powder, cinnamon, 2 tablespoons of the ginger, and walnuts in a medium bowl.

2. Add the egg and butter; mix until just blended. Spread the mixture evenly in the pan. Sprinkle the remaining brown sugar and ginger over the top; press lightly. Bake 30 minutes, or until the top is lightly browned and the edges pull away from the pan. Cool and cut into 16 bars. Pack in an airtight container.

Yields 16 bars

Meditation Tea

Steeped with soothing herbs and spices.

6 cups cold water
2 teaspoons anise seeds
¾ cup fresh mint leaves, bruised with a mortar and pestle
7 teaspoons loose chamomile tea, or 7 tea bags
Juice from one orange, or ⅓ to ½ cup orange juice
3 tablespoons honey, or to taste

Bring the water to a boil. Meanwhile, in a small skillet, toast the anise seeds over medium heat for about 3 minutes, or until lightly browned. Put the mint, anise seeds, and the tea in a large teapot; pour the water over the herbs and steep five minutes. Strain through a fine sieve. Add the orange juice and honey; mix well. Pour into an insulated thermos.

Yields 6½ cups

The scarred aftermath of logging on the east shore of Green Lake in the 1890s. *Museum of History and Industry. Photo by Anders Wilse*

Chapter 10

"Give Back to Green Lake" Buffet

IN RETURN FOR VOLUNTEERING a few hours on the habitat enhancement project, I learned about the native plants of Green Lake from an expert, met neighbors from the other side of the lake, and was given some wild iris bulbs. I felt amply paid for my time. Volunteerism at the lake has a long history. It began in 1905 with the formation of an improvement club after the lake was granted to the city. There was much to be accomplished. The area had been clear-cut and logged, nearly destroying the ecosystem. Present Seattlites would not have recognized the acres of scarred land. Because it is a shallow lake, left alone Green Lake likely would have evolved into a swamp and dried up.

Today, volunteers work year-round to maintain and improve the lake in cooperation with Seattle Parks and Recreation. Despite its size, Green Lake Park has only one gardener. Members of the community are encouraged to take an active role in keeping the park vital, and many do so by participating in work parties sponsored by the city. Held throughout the year, volunteers from Adopt-A-Park gather to plant, prune, rake and weed. Participation is a good way to teach children the value of volunteering and have fun at the same time. For more information about volunteer opportunities with Seattle Parks and Recreation, call 206-233-3979.

One of the key volunteer organizations at the park is the Green Lake Park Alliance (GLPA), founded in 1996. GLPA, a nonprofit organization, has ambitious goals including a master plan for Green Lake. Committees include education, reforestation, and history. GLPA and Seattle Parks and Recreation often partner on special projects. The Alliance also publishes a newsletter, the *Green Lake News*. Articles include updates on GLPA projects, a calendar of community activities, and information about the history and habitat of the lake. The Green Lake Park Alliance is always in need of volunteers for a variety of projects, from planting trees to office support. For a recorded message about upcoming opportunities call 206-985-9235.

Green Lake also has an active community council. Interested residents voice ideas and concerns at the meetings, and keep their pulse on the neighborhood. The council welcomes new members. Membership fees include a subscription to their newsletter *Green Lines.*

Invite your friends to a volunteer work party and afterwards treat them to this Mexican buffet featuring spareribs that will stick with you. Our first trip to Mexico inspired this menu. These recipes blend the flavors of Mexico with just enough bite to be interesting but not overpowering. (We don't include the fiery salsa from Puerto Vallarta, where Carol amused the locals by nearly choking on the salsa.) The finale, *Lemon Heaven Ice with Berries,* is pure and refreshing.

Tomatillo Salsa

Use only fresh tomatillos for this recipe. If unavailable, serve our Nopales Corn Salsa instead.

6 large fresh tomatillos, husks on
1 tablespoon olive oil
½ medium onion, chopped
4 cloves garlic, chopped
2 plum tomatoes, chopped
½ to 1 whole serrano chili pepper, seeded and minced
1 tablespoon fresh lemon juice
1 teaspoon sugar
⅓ cup coarsely chopped cilantro

1. Preheat the oven to 450 degrees. In a small heatproof dish, roast the tomatillos 10 minutes with the husks on. Remove from the oven and cool. Wash, removing the husks and stems; coarsely chop.

2. Meanwhile, in a medium skillet, heat the olive oil over medium heat and sauté the onions until soft, about 5 minutes. Add the garlic and cook briefly. Add the tomatillos, tomatoes, serrano chili, lemon juice, and sugar; cook briefly. Remove from the heat. Stir in the cilantro; add salt and freshly ground pepper to taste. Put in a serving bowl and chill, or serve at room temperature.

Yields about 2 cups

Parmesan Tortilla Triangles

Serve these chips instead of the usual corn tortilla. Add more Tabasco if you like spicy foods. They're best made the same day and served warm from the oven.

¼ cup vegetable oil
¼ teaspoon Tabasco, or to taste
1 teaspoon balsamic vinegar
1 teaspoon onion flakes
10 8-inch flour tortillas
1 cup finely grated Parmesan cheese
Coarse salt (optional)

Preheat the oven to 350 degrees. Whisk the oil, Tabasco, balsamic vinegar, and onion flakes. Lightly brush one tortilla with the oil mixture and sprinkle with cheese. Cut in half and each half into thirds. Repeat with the remaining tortillas. Bake 12 to 15 minutes on a baking sheet, until lightly browned and crisp. Sprinkle lightly with salt.

Yields 60 triangles

Southwestern Caesar Salad

The croutons can be made ahead of time; store in a tightly sealed container.

CROUTONS
⅓ cup olive oil
4 cloves garlic, chopped
½ fresh serrano chili pepper, cut into 4 pieces (remove seeds for milder flavor)
⅛ teaspoon freshly ground pepper
2-inch round demi-baguette or good quality (firm) French bread

CAESAR DRESSING
2 tablespoons fresh lime juice
½ teaspoon dry mustard
2 teaspoons Worcestershire sauce
2 cloves garlic, chopped
1 tablespoon chopped cilantro (optional)
3 rolled anchovies with capers, chopped
⅓ cup olive oil

1 large bunch romaine lettuce, washed, dried, and torn into bite-size pieces
⅓ cup good quality grated Parmesan cheese

1. To make croutons: warm the ⅓ cup olive oil, 4 cloves garlic, serrano chili, and black pepper in a small pan; remove from heat. Let stand 20 minutes to infuse the oil. Meanwhile, slice the baguette into ¼-inch rounds, or remove the crusts from the French bread and cube 2 to 3 cups.

2. Strain the oil into a sauté pan and heat over medium heat. Add the bread and cook until crisp, golden brown, shaking the pan occasionally. Drain on a paper towel. Store in an airtight container.

3. To make dressing: combine the lime juice, mustard, Worcestershire sauce, 2 cloves garlic, cilantro and anchovies in a small bowl. Gradually whisk in the olive oil; add salt and freshly ground pepper to taste.

4. Combine the romaine lettuce, Parmesan cheese, and croutons; dress and serve immediately.

Yields 4 to 6 servings

Stick to Your Ribs

These ribs can be broiled or grilled.

4 pounds boneless country style pork spareribs
1 small onion, chopped
3 cloves garlic, chopped
2 tablespoons vegetable oil
1 or 2 chipotle peppers in adobo sauce, seeded and minced, or ground
  chipotle to taste
2 tablespoons white wine vinegar
2 teaspoons dry mustard
½ teaspoon ground cumin
½ teaspoon chili powder
½ teaspoon ground allspice
¼ teaspoon salt
Generous pinch of freshly ground pepper
1 cup catsup
3 tablespoons brown sugar
Mesquite wood chips, prepared according to package directions

1. Preheat the oven to 350 degrees. Put the ribs in a roasting pan and
    cover; bake 45 minutes. You can cook them a day in advance if desired.
    Cover and refrigerate until ready to grill.

2. Meanwhile, in a medium saucepan, sauté the onion and garlic in the
    vegetable oil over medium-low heat about 10 minutes. Add the chipotle
    peppers, vinegar, mustard, cumin, chili powder, allspice, salt, and pepper.
    Simmer a few more minutes. Add the catsup, brown sugar, and 1 cup
    water; stir well. Simmer about 15 minutes, or until slightly thickened.
    Adjust the seasoning if desired.

3. Prepare the grill. The ribs should be cooked over medium-hot coals.
    When they are ready, add the wood chips. Grill the ribs on an oiled rack
    about 6 inches above the coals, basting with the sauce. Turn occasionally,
    cooking until browned, about 10 minutes. Discard the sauce. Serve
    immediately.

Yields 6 servings

Tropical Fruit and Beans

If you prefer, you can make the beans from scratch. Follow the directions on the package.

1 tablespoon vegetable oil
1 medium onion, chopped
2 cloves garlic, peeled and slightly crushed
½ fresh jalapeño chili pepper, seeded
1 whole cinnamon stick
2 cans (15 ounces each) black beans, undrained
½ cup chopped dried tropical fruit mix (preferably Sunsweet Fruitlings)

In a medium saucepan, heat the oil over medium heat. Add the onion, garlic, jalapeño, and cinnamon stick. Cook until the onions are soft, about 5 minutes. Add the beans and dried fruit; simmer 10 minutes. Add salt and pepper to taste. Remove the garlic, jalapeño, and cinnamon stick. Serve beans immediately.

Yields 6 servings

Lemon Heaven Ice with Berries

This ice does not require an ice cream maker.

4 cups cold water
1½ cups sugar
1½ cups fresh lemon juice (about 8 medium lemons)
2 tablespoons white table wine (optional)
1 cup fresh strawberries or other seasonal berries

1. Bring the water and sugar to a boil in a medium saucepan. Stir until the sugar has dissolved. Remove from the heat and cool. (To cool faster, pour the mixture into another large heatproof pan or bowl.)

2. Add the lemon juice and white wine to the sugar syrup; stir well. Pour the mixture into a large shallow noncorrosive baking pan and carefully place in the freezer. When almost frozen (about 4 hours), remove and break up into small pieces.

3. Process the mixture in a blender or food processor until the texture is like grainy snow. Spoon into a covered container and freeze. Serve in individual bowls with fresh strawberries or other seasonal fruit.

Yields 1½ quarts

Young trees, many planted by volunteers, enhance the lake's shoreline. *Susan Banks*

The Green Lake business district has come a long way since 1911, when this photo was taken. *MSCUA, Univ. of Washington Libraries, Neg. UW 294*

Neighborhood Attractions: A Sampler

Freebies

- Rose Garden at Woodland Park Zoo—800 North 50th Street
  Hundreds of varieties. Take your lunch and relax on a bench.

- Green Lake Public Library—7364 East Green Lake Drive North
  Story time, book discussion groups and more.

- Charming neighborhoods surrounding Green Lake
  Take a stroll through the neighborhoods. You can still see some of the original homes dating from the 1880s. Types of houses include company cottages, Victorian, bungalows, Colonial, California style, Tudor, ranch, and contemporary. For a different view of the area, explore the alleys just off the main street. Feel the crunch of gravel beneath your feet and smell the roses.

Retail Stores

- Gregg's Greenlake Cycle—7007 Woodlawn Avenue Northeast
  A neighborhood icon since 1932.

- Super Jock 'N Jill—7210 East Green Lake Drive North
  One of the best running shops in the city.

- PCC Natural Markets—7504 Aurora Avenue North
  A full service natural foods grocery store.

- Albertson's Food & Drug—6900 East Green Lake Way
  Pick up anything you've forgotten.

Restaurants

Best Bets for Breakfast

- Honey Bear Bakery—2106 North 55th Street
  A good place to meet your friends.

- Urban Bakery—7850 East Green Lake Drive North
  Enjoy the ambiance of the lake from the plaza.

Formal dining

- Nell's—6804 East Green Lake Way North (formerly Saleh al Lago)
  Chef Philip Mihalski worked with Saleh Joudeh before he closed the restaurant in 1999.

- Brie & Bordeaux—2227 North 56th Street
  Visit the wine and cheese shop after you have dinner.

Informal Dining and Take Out

- Duke's Greenlake Chowder House—7850 Green Lake Drive North
  Sample the award-winning chowder with a piece of warm sourdough bread.

- Golden Lake Restaurant—7208 East Green Lake Drive North
  No checks taken, but plenty of good food for a reasonable price.

- Six Degrees—7900 East Green Lake Drive North
  Pub food and microbrews. No one under 21.

- Guidos Pizza—7900 East Green Lake Drive North
  New York-style pizza by the slice.

- Beth's Cafe—7311 Aurora Avenue North
  Home of the 12-egg omelet.

- Spud Fish & Chips—6860 East Green Lake Way North
  Serving up fish and chips since 1948. Near Albertson's.

- Baskin-Robbins—7110 East Green Lake Drive North
  Make this your last stop and buy a quart to go.

Coffee Shops

- Seattle's Best Coffee—6850 East Green Lake Way North
  Across from the east end of the lake. Sit on the sidewalk and watch the world go by.

- Starbucks—7100 East Green Lake Drive North
  Take your newspaper upstairs and relax on the balcony overlooking the lake.

- Tully's Coffee—7900 East Green Lake Drive North
  Sip your coffee in front of the fireplace on a rainy winter day.

Not to Be Missed

- The Woodland Park Zoo—5500 Phinney Avenue North
  Plan to spend the day. Ranked as one of the top ten in the United States.

Selected Bibliography

Dorpat, Paul. 1984. *Seattle, Now & Then*. Seattle: Tartu Publications.

Historic Seattle Preservation and Development Authority. 1975. *An Urban Resource Inventory for Seattle*. Seattle.

Itzkow, Harry and Jane Itzkow. 1987. *The First Twenty-Five Years (1940–1965): A History of the Queen City Lawn Bowling Club*. Harry and Jane Itzkow: Seattle.

Jacobson, Arthur Lee. 1992. *Trees of Green Lake*. Seattle: A. L. Jacobson.

Morgan, Brandt. 1979. *Enjoying Seattle's Parks*. Seattle: Greenwood Publications.

Seattle Public Library, Green Lake Branch. 1994. *The Green Lake Community Archives*. Seattle: Seattle Public Library, Green Lake Branch.

Susan Banks

Susan Banks grew up in Anchorage, Alaska. Her interest in cooking was sparked during college when she worked with Carol in her catering business. After a career in the grocery retail industry, she moved to Washington state. In 1993, Susan earned certificates in Classic Cuisine and Pastry Arts at Le Cordon Bleu in London. Now a librarian, Susan continues to cook for pleasure. She resides at Green Lake with her husband, Stewart.

Carol Orr

Carol Orr became interested in cooking as a teenager while traveling with her mother through Europe. Her passion for travel and cooking remains a primary source of curiosity and pleasure. She has lived in Italy and Japan, studying the local foods. Professionally, she has co-owned a catering business, taught cooking classes, and worked as a chef and baker. Carol and her husband, David, live with their two daughters in Hillsboro, Oregon.